Kids Eat

NEW YORK

The Essential Guide to Family-Friendly Restaurants in New York City

SAM FREUND & ELIZABETH CARPENTER

(A Kid & His Mom)

THE LITTLE BOOKROOM
New York

Acknowledgments

The authors would like to give special thanks to the many people who helped us with this book, especially Adrienne Hartman, Ellen Williams and Margaret Meyers.

And to the many wonderful restaurateurs whose establishments we have described in this book, we applaud you for your kid-friendliness.

© 1997 by Elizabeth Carpenter and Sam Freund
Cover Illustration © 1997 by Adrienne Hartman
Book Design: © 1997 by Elizabeth Carpenter

ISBN 0-9641262-4-9
Library of Congress Catalog Card Number:
97-71866
First printing: July 1997

Published by The Little Bookroom
5 St. Luke's Place
New York, NY 10014
(212) 691-3321
Fax (212) 691-2011

TABLE OF CONTENTS

●●●●●●●●●●●●●●●●●●●●●●●●●●●●●●●●

KIDS EAT NEW YORK

4

GUIDE TO SYMBOLS

• •

SYMBOL GUIDE

Note: Slashed symbols indicate this option not avavailable.

SYMBOL   DESCRIPTION

Subway directions

Reservations accepted
Number+ (example: 6+) indicates
reservation minimum

**American Express, MasterCard,
& VISA credit cards accepted.**
AMEX only indicates only American
Express accepted.
No AMEX indicates American
Express not accepted.

Kids' menu available

Milk available
If you don't see it on the menu – ask.

Suitable for small children

**Hi-chairs or booster seats
available**

Strollers welcome

Wheelchair accessible

**Wheelchair accessible
rest rooms**

STAR BALLOONS SYMBOLS

The most important thing about each restaurant is how well we liked it, and so we invented the **STAR BALLOON** symbol. (If a restaurant didn't rate any balloons, we decided not to include it in this book.)

1 STAR BALLOON means that the restaurant is OK.

2 STAR BALLOONS mean that it is a good place, better than OK, worth going back to.

3 STAR BALLOONS mean that it is very good and we think that kids would be happy if the grown-ups decided to go there.

4 STAR BALLOONS mean that it is a great place and we definitely like to tell our friends about this place.

5 STAR BALLOONS are reserved for fantastic restaurants, really special places where kids and parents feel very lucky to go.

PRICE RANGE SYMBOL GUIDE

We are using a dollar (**$**) symbol system to identify the price range of each restaurant. The range is determined by dividing a total dinner bill, including non-alcoholic drinks, tips, and tax, by the number of diners, kids and adults.

Under $ 15/person:	Inexpensive	**$**
$15 - 30/person:	Moderate	**$$**
$30 - 50/person:	Expensive	**$$$**
Over $50/person:	Very Expensive	**$$$$**

INTRODUCTION
by Mimi Sheraton

• •

"Are there any restaurants that we can go to with children?"

That is one of the questions most frequently asked of restaurant critics, especially in our large cities where the high cost of operation makes curmudgeons of even the kindest restaurateurs. Not only are they wary of offending adult customers by seating them near children who might be noisy and wander in the aisles, but they worry about being asked to provide half-portions at reduced prices and for special adjustments in food preparation, especially during peak hours.

Implied in that frequent question, of course, is the wish for meals that will be acceptable to adults, ruling out such obvious choices as national fast food chains. Fortunately, New York offers a wide range of better options from small local chains with inexpensive, decent and diverting food to full-fledged white-tablecloth restaurants with serious kitchens and equally serious prices for special occasions. (With the latter, it is devoutly to be wished that families with children under ten would be finished with dinner by 7:30.)

The problem is selecting the right child-friendly restaurant for a given meal, in terms of location, price, type of food and degree of formality. The decision also depends on the age, level of sophistication, threshold of crankiness, and to some extent, the gender of the children involved. Sugar and spice and fancy frills that appeal to most little girls, might give little boys nothing but the giggles, or worse.

9

KIDS EAT NEW YORK

Enter Elizabeth Carpenter, her 10-year-old son, Sam Freund, and assorted friends of all ages, who tirelessly ate their way through a reported 500 meals to come up with more than 150 answers to the above questions.

Typically where New York is concerned, there are surprises, even to one who has been a restaurant critic in this city for over twenty-five years. I expected to find entertaining and savory options such as the inexpensive Ollie's Noodle Shops, various museum restaurants, the lusty Brooklyn Diner and Mickey Mantle's with all of its baseball memorabilia, but the good and stylish Arqua and Odeon, and the operatic Layla with its delicious Middle Eastern food, musical comedy decor and amusing belly dancers might not have occurred to me.

The diligent authors have thought of just about everything that will help confused parents make a choice. They include details such as the availability of half-portions and kids' menus, high chairs and booster seats, milk, and diversions for the young and the restless. That in addition to standard guide-book facts such as the credit cards accepted, hours, transportation directions, and more. There are also nicely written introductory descriptions of each restaurant, delineating overall mood so that one knows exactly what to expect. Judging from those descriptions of the restaurants I know well, the authors are extremely accurate. They almost convince me that taking children to restaurants can be fun, and that's saying a lot for this original and entertaining work.

Mimi Sheraton, former restaurant critic for *The New York Times*, writes regularly about food for *Condé Nast Traveler* and other publications. She is the author of numerous cookbooks.

To Rick, Tracy, Danny, and Nicholas, for their love and unfailing support (and for visiting and revisiting so many restaurants with us), and to Mark Freund, who was always with us in spirit.

WHY WE WROTE THIS BOOK

I like to go out to eat with my friends and our parents, but a lot of the restaurants my mom likes either are boring or don't really like kids (or both). We are always on the lookout for places where I can have a good time and the food is good enough for the grown-ups, especially since my mom doesn't like junk food.

This book is a list of restaurants that we like a lot and think that kids and their families should try. Mostly we like places where there is something going on, but we always like places that are friendly to kids and have food that is not too fancy. We wrote this book so kids would know where to go eat in New York City, but don't worry, parents, my mom double-checked all the details.

SAM FREUND
Age 11
New York City, 1997

As a busy New York City mother, I sometimes need a break from the hectic pace of life in the city. Restaurants offer a chance to relax and enjoy the company of family and friends. But as all parents know, most Manhattan restaurants are not great places to take kids (or so I thought). Like everyone else, I found myself going back to the same reliable spots rather than chance *dining disaster*. But what if you find yourself with your family in another part of town at mealtime? What if you want to try someplace new?

In a city filled with great restaurants, we searched

unsuccessfully for a guidebook that focused on the dining needs of kids aged two to 12, let alone kids and parents. So, as they say, we wrote the book.

In each review, we have tried to convey a sense of the atmosphere, friendliness, service, decor, and entertainment appeal, as well as describe what's on the menu. For us, a wonderful place to eat is not necessarily the most trendy; nor does it have to serve gourmet food. But the setting must be a place where we all have a good time, and the food has to be thoughtfully prepared. After sampling and eliminating many places where the food was sub-standard, the service snobby, or the whole experience boring, Sam and I have agreed on more than 150 restaurants that meet both our criteria: they must be kid-friendly and parent-worthy.

To ensure that you know as much as possible in advance, we've included information about hours, cost and credit cards, and whether restaurants serve milk, supply high chairs, provide wheelchair access, accommodate strollers, have a kids' menu, and are suitable for young children. We've also evaluated the on-site restaurants of most of the city's major attractions for kids and identified nearby dining alternatives.

While considerable effort has been made to verify the accuracy of all the information in this book, restaurants in New York City are constantly changing. Therefore, we suggest that you always call ahead.

We hope that you find this book valuable and that you refer to it often. If there are any additions that you feel should be included in future editions, please contact us in care of our publisher, The Little Bookroom, 5 Saint Luke's Place, NY, NY 10014 and we will consider any suggestions.

From our family to yours, whether you're from Manhattan, Milwaukee or Milan, cheers!

ELIZABETH CARPENTER
New York City, 1997

P.S. Living in New York City we are surrounded by a multitude of significant cultural, historic, and educational attractions that are great to experience with children. Unfortunately the majority of guides to these special attractions are not written for families. Because we know your time is at a premium, we have included information how to successfully navigate as a family 12 of the most important attractions, including dining options, eliminating the need to carry a second guidebook for at least a dozen outings. In the indexes we have also recommended nearby restaurants for many other attractions your family may wish to visit.

TIPS TO ENSURE A PLEASANT TIME

● ●

1. GO EARLY

Most restaurants open for dinner between 5 and 6 PM; their customers don't usually start to show up, however, until 7 or 7:30. This is convenient for families because kids get hungry for dinner when restaurants are the most empty, yet have a full staff on duty. Even trendy places such as the Bowery Bar often are friendly to kids then — after all, they represent business a restaurant would not ordinarily have. And the staff at restaurants that are usually friendly to kids have the time to relax and serve you even better.

2. CALL AHEAD

If you are concerned about waiting when you arrive at a restaurant, by all means call. You may spare your family disappointment, especially during peak dining hours. And many establishments that don't take reservations may do their best to accommodate you if you tell them that you are bringing children.

3. BRING ENTERTAINMENT

No matter what other diversions a restaurant may offer, I always bring back-up entertainment. Depending on what activities Sam is into at the moment, my satchel may contain coloring and drawing materials, card games, a GAME BOY, books, and even homework.

4. BE SPECIFIC WHEN ORDERING
(and send it back if it's not right.)

If there is anything special about how you want your meals prepared, be specific and confirm that it is possible. If you are not satisfied with your food, be nice about it, but don't hesitate to send it back. That said, I must admit that I am guilty of having picked a lot of parsley and shredded basil off Sam's plates during his lifetime.

5. IF YOUR CHILD IS TIRED OR SICK, GO HOME

There is no point pushing an upset child into a restaurant situation, especially if it's supposed to be enjoyable and you're paying for it. As a parent, you know whether or not your kid is cranky because he or she is hungry or whether the problem is more serious. If hunger is the issue, by all means, get that child something to eat! It never fails to amaze me how quickly kids can metabolize their food — they're down in the dumps one minute and full of zip the next. Which brings me to my last tip.

6. ORDER THE CHILDREN'S MEALS FIRST, TO BE SERVED AS SOON AS READY

Let the adults take their time pondering what to order — but don't wait to place your kids' requests. After all, as all parents know, happy kids at the dinner table make for a happier meal for everyone.

DOWNTOWN, CHINATOWN & TRIBECA

• •

The **Downtown** area runs from the southernmost tip of Manhattan to Chambers Street and includes Wall Street and the financial district, the World Trade Center towers, Battery Park City, and the South Street Seaport.

Chinatown is roughly located east of Broadway and south of Canal Street, in the area around the Brooklyn Bridge.

The acronym **TriBeCa** means the triangle below Canal Street that is bounded by Chambers Street to the south, Church Street to the east, and the Hudson River to the west. TriBeCa is a neighborhood in transition as its commercial and industrial buildings are renovated into spacious residential lofts.

RESTAURANTS

ATTRACTIONS with RESTAURANTS

ARQUA

281 Church St. (at White St.)

(334-1888

A,C,E,N,R,4,5,6 to Canal St.;
1,9 to Franklin St.

Hours:
Lunch: Mon-Fri: 12 noon - 3 PM
Dinner:
Mon-Thu: 5 - 10 PM
Fri & Sat: 5 - 11:30 PM
Sun: 5 - 10 PM.
(Sun: closed in late summer)
Brunch: Sat/Sun: 11 AM - 3 PM

$$$ **Entertainment:** No

It is always a treat when an absolutely stunning meal can be a full family affair. Arqua is truly a standout — in beauty, in quality, and in spirit. The decor of the restaurant is simple yet elegant. Up a few steps from the street, the room has high ceilings and warm earth-toned walls, unadorned except for Italian-designed light fixtures. A magnificent floral display cascades from a large urn centered on a column. The large tables with white linens are nicely spaced and conversation is the music of the room, so kids can talk freely.

A quiet fixture in TriBeCa for almost a decade, this small restaurant specializes in Venetian cuisine, with an emphasis on seafood. The owners were born in Italy and have strong family ties there, allowing them to visit often and gather new recipes regularly. Most of the kitchen and the wait staff are also of Mediterranean descent. Arqua is a perfect place to celebrate a special occasion, and, while expensive, the meal will also be a celebration for your taste buds.

Be sure to ask about the unpublished $8.95 children's menu. Your little ones can choose from pasta with butter or red sauce, roasted free-range chicken, and sometimes a daily special just for kids. A big bowl of either vanilla or chocolate gelato, chocolate cake, or Italian cheesecake comes with the kids' meal. Soda or milk is served in a wine glass, which Sam thought was elegant.

For the adults, we suggest starting your meal with the Cozze Aglio Olio (sautéed mussels), or the Salsiccia Della Casa (grilled chicken and mushroom sausage). You can also select your starter from the daily specials: the unique seafood risotto custard is heavenly, as is the salmon carpaccio. You can also order a sampling from the tempting antipasti display located at the front of the restaurant.

The pasta is made fresh daily on the premises. Select from pesto taglierini, the traditional pasta al frutti di mare (shellfish in a red sauce), or the daily ravioli, among other choices. In addition to the superb seared tuna or the zuppa di pesce (fish and shellfish soup), we recommend the rack of lamb in balsamic vinegar, and the roasted, thinly-sliced veal. Dinner prices are quite steep, with salads and appetizers averaging $9, the pastas $16 and the main dishes $20 to $24. Be sure to ask your waiter for the details of the weekday $25 prix fixe option, which includes soup or salad, a half portion of pasta, and a selection of entrees, among them the excellent roasted free-range chicken. (A $20 prix fixe lunch is also available.) There is a full bar, a good American and Italian wine list, and a nice selection of beautifully presented desserts. The impeccable service is friendly, there when needed, never pushy. The owners have two school-aged children, and are extremely accommodating to kids. Keep Arqua in mind when planning a very special family occasion such as a graduation, or birthday.

BUBBY'S
120 Hudson St. (at N. Moore St.)

(219-0666

🚇 1,9 to Franklin St.

Hours:
Breakfast:
Mon-Fri: 9 AM - 4 PM
Lunch/Dinner:
Mon-Fri: 11 AM - 10 PM
Sat & Sun: 6 - 10 PM
Brunch: Sat/Sun: 9 AM - 5 PM

 $-$$ **Entertainment:** No

Bubby's is a easygoing neighborhood restaurant where the locals love the food (and the low prices) so much that they don't seem to mind the inefficient air conditioner or the strictly industrial scenery. The blues and jazz recordings and the 1940s and 1950s kitsch photos, toys, and bric-a-brac make this restaurant feel as if it could be located in the artsy neighborhoods of many American cities. Though unpretentious, somehow you know that your fellow diners, seated at the simple wooden tables and chairs, are very hip and involved in artistic endeavors of great importance.

Popular with families, Bubby's can be very busy at the weekend brunches. It is a little quieter during the week and street parking is no problem. Rumor has it that Bubby's started out as a pie shop, and grew into a restaurant one recipe at a time. While there is no specific kids' menu, many things on the regular menu, which can be cooked "plain" or in half portions, will certainly appeal to children. The eclectic American cuisine includes soups and salads, appetizers (grown-ups, try the fried baby artichokes), basic and gourmet sandwiches and burgers, pastas such as the roasted pine nut pesto, and entrees like pan-seared Thai salmon and rosemary chicken. There are blackboard specials as well. Beverages include homemade sodas (plus the regular ones), shakes, malts, floats, fresh juices, wine, beer, coffee and tea. And don't forget to leave room for those pies and cakes, which can be ordered whole to take home (call in advance) or by the slice.

ELLEN'S CAFE AND BAKE SHOP
270 Broadway (at Chambers St.)

(962-1257

4,5,6,N,R to City Hall; 2,3 to Park Pl.; A,C to Chambers St.

Hours:
Mon-Fri: 6 AM- 7 PM
Sat: 8 AM - 4 PM
Sun: Closed
Brunch: No

Entertainment: No

Ellen's Cafe and Bake Shop has for 30 years been a pleasant oasis in the hustle and bustle of the City Hall area. More than just a coffee shop, it is decorated in an Art Nouveau speakeasy style, with ornate wall lamps and chandeliers, and tall mirrors etched with turn-of-the-century designs of people, carriages, and sailing vessels. You can sit at either a booth, a table, or at one of the sandwich counters, which swing out in large "U" shapes and have swivel stools. Ellen Hart, who also owns Ellen's Stardust Diner and Dine-O-Mat, was the winner of the 1959 Miss Subways beauty pageant, and photos of her with various celebrities, of other Miss Subways, and of their reunions decorate the walls.

The menu is extensive but not expensive. Indeed, it is hard to find any item listed for more than $10. Choices that might appeal to kids include grilled cheese, burgers, fish and chips, fried chicken, and macaroni and cheese (Mondays only). Also served are great wide French fries, a variety of soups, salads, sandwiches, omelets, fajitas, and seafood. The food is reliable and the portions are large.

Drinks include shakes, ice cream sodas, egg creams, sodas, milk, juice, lemonade, coffee, and a full bar. And if you have room, you can check out the desserts in the front display case. The service is no more or less than required, and the staff welcomes children of all ages.

GOLDEN UNICORN

18 E. Broadway (at Catherine St.)

(941-0911

🚇 4,5,6 to Brooklyn Bridge;
J,M,Z to Chambers St.;
B,D,Q to Grand St.

Hours:
Mon-Fri: 9 AM - 10 PM
Sat & Sun: 8:30 AM - 10:30 PM
Brunch: No

💳 $-$$

Entertainment: Dim sum carts

One of the great things about New York is the enormous diversity of cuisines. The opportunities for Chinese food in New York are especially plentiful, and dim sum is one of the more entertaining eating experiences for kids. Dim sum, which is sort of an endless parade of hors d'oeuvres, is served from carts pushed from table to table. The typical vast restaurants that serve dim sum are a circus of activity, noise, smells and textures.

Among the best-known of these palaces is Golden Unicorn. Located in the middle of Chinatown, the restaurant's dining rooms are on two upstairs floors in an unimpressive-looking office building.

KIDS EAT NEW YORK

Once escorted to a table through the crowded dining rooms, diners immediately start choosing from the constantly-circulating carts. Grilled beef, sticky rice with chicken, and sweet and sour pork are all simple items that most children like. Then perhaps you can try the spring rolls, fried wontons, and the crystal fried rice.

When everyone has satisfied his immediate hunger, the fun really starts. A cart of bamboo steamers is wheeled by, one containing dumplings … and inside the dumplings, who knows? Hardly any of the women pushing the carts speaks any English at all, so we simply point to different foods and try them without any real idea of what we're getting. But the individual items are so small and priced so low, you are encouraged to sample a feast of unknown foods. We discovered shrimp balls, sweet pork buns and grilled shrimp in the shell — messy to peel but delicious. We passed on the preserved duck eggs, the white custard and the chicken feet. Although the service can be as chaotic as the room, most families enjoy the experience. Then walk a few blocks through Chinatown — it will only add to your adventure.

HAMBURGER HARRY'S

157 Chambers St.
(between Hudson & Greenwich Sts.)

☎ 267-4446
🚇 1,2,3,9,A,C to Chambers St.

Hours:
Mon-Fri: 11:30 AM - 10 PM
Sat: 12 noon - 9 PM
Sun: Closed
Brunch: No

Entertainment: No

Note: On Saturdays KIDS EAT FREE.

There are two Hamburger Harry's, once both owned by the same person. Today they are owned and run separately and have different but similar menus. Both are good places to take kids.

With a name like Hamburger Harry's, it's no surprise that the focus of this place is burgers. This restaurant is relatively small with butcher block tables and a very accommodating attitude. You can watch the burgers, which include vegetable and salmon options, being grilled over mesquite wood and charcoal in the open circular kitchen. Other menu items include tacos and fajitas, salads, sandwiches and chili. Available beverages are milk, soda, wine and beer, as well as milkshakes and floats. Ice cream, Mississippi mudcake, and apple or three-berry pie are among the desserts.

Ask about the children's menu because they don't have a printed one. For kids 11 years old and younger, chicken nuggets are $2.49 and cheeseburgers are $2.99, and a child-sized portion of anything from the adult menu is half price.

On Saturdays, one kid per paying adult can eat for free, and anyone who is a student (bring an ID if you are an adult) can order the student special, which is a small burger, fries, and a soda for $2.99.

HUDSON GRILL

350 Hudson St. (at King St.)

📞 691-9060

🚇 1,9 to Houston St.

Hours:

Mon-Fri (only): 11:30 AM - 10 PM

Sat & Sun: Closed

Brunch: No

💳 $

Entertainment: Games, pool table

Located in an area filled mainly with office buildings, the Hudson Grill amply fulfills the neighborhood's need for good food at reasonable prices. Strictly a weekday operation, it does a large business serving the people in the nearby brokerage firms, publishing houses and ad agencies. In addition, it provides catering services to the likes of MTV. The restaurant itself is a combination bar, eatery, and art gallery; in the evenings, comedy and variety shows are staged in an upstairs lounge. We prefer sitting on the side of the dining room that has walls painted in bright Necco wafer colors and large windows that overlook King Street.

Although there is a good-sized lunch crowd, it is much quieter in the evenings, and reservations are not necessary.

The menu, which is the same for lunch and dinner, is a collection of tried-and-true favorites, all inexpensive. Appetizers include buffalo wings, nachos, and potato skins. There are at least a dozen types of salads, and an even larger list of pastas. Entrees include chicken, steak, shrimp, fish and chips, and tuna steak. If that isn't enough, there are omelets, burgers, burritos (the beef burrito is filled with strip steak), stir fry, and BBQ. Bring five or more friends for a birthday celebration and the birthday person's entree is on the house.

Sam likes coming here for several reasons. First, because they have a pool table, which is well lit and not at all seedy. Second, because they have a large assortment of board games such as Scrabble, Pictionary, backgammon, and chess that you can play at your table. He likes the rock music playing in the background (Eagles to Zeppelin to rap), but most important, he likes the friendly staff members who occasionally stop by with a game-clinching tip... such as a 30 point Scrabble word.

LAYLA

211 W. Broadway (at Franklin St.)

☎ 431-0700

🚇 N,R to Canal St.

Hours:
Lunch:
Mon-Fri: 12 noon - 2:30 PM
Dinner:
Mon-Thu: 5:30 - 10:45 PM
Fri & Sat: 5:30 - 11:15 PM
Sun: 5:30 - 10 PM
Brunch: No

 $$$

Entertainment:
Belly dancer after 9 PM

Layla charmed us from the moment we walked in. It's like stepping into an Arabian Nights film set, in which every detail is well thought out and beautifully executed. Exotic 3-D tile dioramas, including one of a snake charmer plying his trade, decorate the walls. Cobalt blue bottles behind the bar contrast with golden lemons in relief against Arabic tiles. Faux alabaster columns reach to the antiqued ceiling, and pomegranate-colored lamps cast a diffused light on the dark wood tables. A bowl of olives marinated in Moroccan oils, a pouch of flat pita, grilled Zaatar breads, and a dish of creamy garlic dip awaited us as we sat down in the colonial-style caned chairs.

The food here is so good that it is impossible to recommend only a few dishes. As starters, we especially like the lamb ravioli with yogurt mint sauce and the tenderly grilled octopus salad over potatoes and curried apples. If you love full-flavored spicy food, the shellfish couscous will delight you. There's a coriander-crusted filet mignon, and the apricot-glazed lamb kebob, with its fruity sweetness offset by smoky spices, made me think of desert tents and Persian rugs. Kids will like the Zaatar chicken, the grilled shrimp kebobs, the roast codfish, and the filet mignon. The kitchen is happy to prepare dishes "simply" and will substitute homemade potato chips if the exotic side dishes are too adventurous for your child. Service is superb and well-behaved kids are made to feel quite welcome.

The arrival of the bikini-clad belly dancer was perfectly timed, just as we were in between dinner and dessert. With cymbals on her fingers and rings on her toes, she twirled her way through the restaurant. Stopping at our table, she wound a silk scarf around Sam's head and asked, "Will you dance with me?" Sam is still talking about this. Layla is an expensive night out, but for that very special occasion, it's an enchanting evening.

ODEON

145 W. Broadway (at Thomas St.)

☎ 233-0507
🚇 1,9, to Franklin St.

Hours:
Lunch: Mon-Fri: 12 noon - 3 PM
Brunch:
Sat & Sun: 11:30 AM - 4 PM
Dinner: 6 PM - 12 midnight
Brassiere Menu:
3 - 6 PM; and 12 midnight - 3 AM

▬ $$ **Entertainment:** No

Whether it's delivering a superb meal to adults or a simple dish to children, this great TriBeCa brasserie is consistently stylish and alluring. Reminiscent of brasseries in France, the Odeon is dominated at one end by a magnificent Deco bar. The paper-covered tables and banquettes are arranged a little close, so come early if you are bringing four- to six-year-olds, or else reserve a booth.

We have enjoyed every dish we have had from the American/French menu. Appetizers range from classic paté, smoked salmon, and tuna tartare to salads and grilled artichokes. Entrees include pastas (fettuccine with morels and asparagus), grilled vegetable plates, fish (seared tuna with wasabi), and meat dishes (grilled chicken, pepper steak). The children's menu includes burgers, hot dogs, chicken nuggets, pizza, and pasta with sauce or butter. In addition to desserts on the children's menu, we recommend the profiteroles and the classic crème brûlée.

Service is fast and accommodating to children. There is a full bar and a thoughtful wine list. We especially recommend the Odeon for a celebration or dinner with grandparents.

Note: Odeon isn't suitable for infants and toddlers, except for lunch at the outdoor cafe.

SCREENING ROOM

54 Varick St. (at Canal St.)

☎ 334-2100

🚇 1,9,A,C,E to Canal St.

Hours:
Light Breakfast:
In theater coffee bar lobby starting at 7:30 AM
Lunch: 12 noon - 3 PM
Dinner: 5:30 PM - 12 midnight
Brunch: Sun: 11 AM - 4 PM

💳 $$-$$$ **Entertainment:** Yes — Movie theater next door

The Screening Room provides an evening's entertainment — a meal and a film — in a location that captures the spirit of bygone movie palaces of the forties. The restaurant and adjoining theater are furnished with many restored originals, including a mahogany bar and 134 theater seats, seven of which are double "love seats." The restaurant also features humorous details like a curved padded ceiling (which Sam describes as a couch on the ceiling), and squiggly-patterned carpet and upholstery. Three small screening rooms will soon (as of this writing) be available for private parties, one of them an Alice in Wonderland setting.

The restaurant has the hip and casual ambiance of the TriBeCa filmmaking scene. The dress code encompasses everything from jeans to trendy European outfits. Service is excellent, and the knowledgeable staff bends over backward to make kids feel at home. The unprinted kids' menu includes thick hamburgers that come with a mountain of fries, macaroni and cheese, and sandwiches like grilled cheese. The kitchen will make half orders of pasta, and any of the entrees, such as the grilled tuna, shell steak, or chicken, can be prepared plain.

The chef, Mark Spangenthal, a graduate of the kitchen at the Gotham Bar & Grill, is a key attraction here. He has developed a menu of beautifully presented gourmet treats. Adults, don't miss the warm grilled artichoke salad with a reduced sauce or the smoked trout with chicory, and horseradish vinaigrette. For entrees, we suggest the flavorful cedar-planked salmon over braised Swiss chard, and the rich and tender grilled duck, served with a chickpea and chili hominy. Coming to the Screening Room for dessert and the movies is also popular (you can buy your tickets from your waiter), and we wouldn't want to miss the strawberry pie with coconut almond ice cream or the individual lemon "ice box" with local blueberries topped with meringue. As the prices here are high, we suggest reserving the Screening Room for those special events when a chic, sophisticated meal is in order.

SOUTH STREET SEAPORT
Fulton & Water Sts. at Piers 15 - 17 (East River)

• •

☎ Marketplace General Information: 732-7678
☎ South Street Seaport Museum:
  669-9424/669-9400
☎ Liberty Seaport Cruises: 630-8888

TRANSPORTATION:

🚇 2,3,4,5,J,Z,M to Fulton St.
  A,C to Broadway/Nassau St.

Bus:
M15 (South Ferry signs) 2nd Ave. to Fulton St.

Free bus:
NY Waterway provides a complimentary bus service that runs from the World Financial Center to the South Street Seaport every five to ten minutes along the "downtown bus loop route" from 10 AM to 10 PM on the weekends and from 7 AM to 10 PM during the week. The buses are either jitney vans or regular buses. All are painted bright red, white and blue, and have huge "W" signs on the sides. You can hail the buses (just as you would hail a taxi) anywhere along the route and you can take the bus back from the South Street Seaport as well. Call 800-533-3779 for more information.

Note: The red double-decker commercial tour buses stop at the seaport. Check with your tour bus company for details.

Automobile: FDR Drive to South Street exit (#3 southbound, #1 northbound). Follow South Street to Pier 17.

Parking: Easily available in fee-based lots surrounding the seaport.

Taxis: Generally available along South Street and at the taxi stand at Fulton and Water Streets.

KIDS EAT NEW YORK

Even on the hottest day in Manhattan, your family can keep its cool by catching the sea breezes at the South Street Seaport. Restored in the late 1970s under the direction of Boston architects Jane and Ben Thompson, the seaport is spread out over three East River piers, and is also the crossroads of Fulton and Front Streets, from South Street to Water Street, Beekman to John Streets. Included in this area are several historic tall ships, an outdoor performance area, museums, and a collection of shops and restaurants complete with historic buildings and cobblestone streets lined with barrels of flowering plants.

THE PIERS

One of our favorite things is to explore the tall ships docked at Pier 16 (and Pier 15, when open). The ships are set up as self-guided museum tours with informative displays and a movie below deck. Kids are allowed to roam free, under parental supervision, so playing pirate is big for Sam and his friends. The ticket to visit the ships is $2 for adults; kids are free. We have also found the upper deck of the *Peking* to have a great view of the concert stage located between Piers 16 and 17. The concerts and events staged regularly at the seaport are free (call 732-7678 for information). Seaport Liberty conducts scheduled sightseeing and music cruises (630-8888 for times and fees), and you can also sail away on the Seaport Museum's schooner *Pioneer* (669-9400). The South Street Seaport Museum operates two museum stores, one on Pier 16 and one at 12-14 Fulton Street, that sell nautical gifts and books reflective of both the museum's exibits and the historical concept of the port of New York as the focus of commerce and importing for the area.

The Pier 17 Marketplace pavilion is really a three-level shopping mall, which can mean either a good time or immediate parental torture depending on the mood of your little ones. The Marketplace supports an assortment of outside street performers — jugglers, mime artists, and musicians — who, along with the knickknack carts, create quite a festive scene. On the ground floor outside deck is an assortment of food carts selling snacks like Italian ices, hot dogs, and lemonade. Within the Marketplace are many eateries ranging from ice cream shops and the familiar Pizzeria Uno to the four restaurants listed below. The food and service at these kid-friendly restaurants are good but not remarkable. And the prices are higher than they should be, though the views afforded from these pier locations are a real treat.

In addition, there is an inexpensive fast-food court located on the third floor for burgers, pizza, grilled foods (chicken, hot dogs), salads, and seafood, as well as Greek, Chinese, and Cajun specialties. Some of the stands offer $2.98 children's meals. What separates this food court from all others is its very clean seating area, which boasts sweeping water views.

LIBERTY CAFE & OYSTER BAR

3rd Floor, Pier 17

 406-1111

Hours:
Lunch: 10:30 AM - 5 PM
Brunch: Sun: 11 AM - 3 PM
Dinner: 5 PM - 2 AM

 $-$$ **Entertainment:** The seaport

Our favorite restaurant at the seaport is the Liberty Cafe, which has a stunning view of the historic tall ships against a backdrop of skyscrapers, with all the activity of the seaport buzzing below. Very kid friendly, dress is casual. We try to get a table outside in the summer. The American cuisine emphasizes seafood, although the $5.95 children's menu offers fried chicken and fish, burgers, hot dogs, grilled cheese, and PB&J. All are served with fries or chips (except the hot dogs, which come with baked beans) and an ice cream sundae. Daily seafood specials include blackened swordfish with sesame guacamole and an Asian BBQ sauce, and monkfish prepared with roasted red peppers. Among the delicious seafood salads is the grilled calamari, and the seafood ceviche is marinated with daikon and cucumbers. In addition, there are burgers and pizza from a wood-burning oven and meat dishes such as sirloin steak and grilled chicken breast. In addition to a full bar, they offer milk and shakes. And don't forget to save room for the unique Hot Fudge Sundae Pizza — that's right, Sundae Pizza. It's big enough for four hungry kids, and is made of cinnamon-dough shaped like a pizza topped with three flavors of ice cream (chocolate, vanilla, and strawberry), loads of hot fudge sauce, whipped cream and cherries.

SEQUOIA

1st & 2nd Floors, Pier 17

☎ 732-9090

Hours:
11:30 AM - 12 midnight
(Winter closing may be earlier due to weather.)

Brunch:
Sat & Sun: 11:30 AM - 4 PM

$$ \text{—} \quad \$\$ \qquad \textbf{Entertainment: The seaport} $$

This large two-story restaurant at the south end of Pier 17 features indoor and outdoor dining with views of the downtown and Brooklyn skylines and the Brooklyn Bridge. An upscale casual restaurant, the cuisine is American with the emphasis on seafood. Menu highlights include pan-sautéed rainbow trout stuffed with oysters, crabmeat, tomatoes, and spinach and the cioppino, a combination of lobster, clams, mussels, scallops, and calamari in a delicious, slightly spicy tomato broth that is great for dunking bread. Other seafood options include mahimahi and tuna steak au poivre, as well as meat entrees such as lamb chops, steak, and chicken. While there isn't a separate kids' menu, they also serve pizzas, burgers, half orders of pasta (upon request), chicken wings, great fries, and milk. The weekend brunch with omelets, waffles, and pancakes is also nice.

SGARLATO'S CAFE

3rd Floor, Pier 17

 (619-5226

Hours:
Lunch: 11 AM - 4 PM
Brunch:
Sat & Sun: 11 AM - 2 PM
Dinner:
Sun-Thu: 4 PM - 9 or 10 PM
Fri & Sat: 4 PM - 12 midnight

 $$ **Entertainment:** The seaport

Note: Lollipops for good kids

This Italian restaurant, with northern harbor views of the FDR Drive, the East River, and the Brooklyn Bridge has indoor and outdoor dining, and features seafood, pastas, sandwiches, and burgers. Sam and his friends find the menu fascinating because it is in seven languages. The $4.95 to $6.95 kids' menu offers pizza, spaghetti, ravioli, burgers, and chicken fingers. Milk, juice, and sodas are served, and there is a full bar.

PEDRO O'HARA'S

1st Floor, Pier 17

☎ 227-6735

Hours:
11:30 AM - 10:30 PM to 2 AM
(depending on the crowd)
Brunch: No

 $-$$ **Entertainment:** The seaport

Pedro's is a Tex-Mex cafe with indoor and outdoor seating. It's touristy in feel but an easy place for a quick sit-down meal at the edge of all the activity. The menu includes burgers, grilled cheese, BBQ chicken wings, and pizzas from plain to Tex-Mex varieties, as well as tacos, fajitas, quesadillas, and catfish po'boys.

FULTON STREET AREA

● ●

Crossing South Street (under the FDR Drive) to Fulton Street, you'll find the equally lively and interesting other half of the seaport. The reconstructed Fulton Market Building (circa 1882) houses the Fulton Street Cafe (see review below), the Seaport Museum's Boat Building Shop, and the historic Fulton Fish Market (of which you can take a 6 AM walking tour — call 748-8590). People watching from the cafes and benches that line Fulton Street is a fun event in and of itself. There is usually an assortment of street performers ranging from young classical musicians to jugglers and clowns. The steady stream of humanity promenading down Fulton Street is also quite a scene, especially against the backdrop of the large sailing ships in the harbor.

FULTON STREET CAFE

11 Fulton St. (between South and Ferry Sts.)

(227-2288

Summer Hours:
Sun-Thu: 11:30 AM - 9 or 10 PM
Fri & Sat:
11:30 AM - 12 midnight
Winter Hours:
11:30 AM - 8 PM
Brunch: No

 $$ **Entertainment:**
Fulton St., the view

Adjacent to the fish market, this cafe is known for its prime selection of seafood and its raw bar. Check out the chowders, fresh fish sandwiches, seafood salads, and grilled fish. You won't be disappointed by the quality, though the prices reflect the touristy location. Also offered are burgers and hot dogs, pasta, chicken, and steak. There is milk, juice, lemonade, sodas, a selection of beers and ales, and wine. Inside you can watch the chefs preparing the seafood, and the walls have neat paintings of large fish underwater. We prefer to sit outside at the tables shaded by the oversized green market umbrellas so that we can watch all the street action.

CAFE FLEDERMAUS
1 Seaport Plaza (on Fulton St. at Front St.)

☎ 269-5890

Hours:
7 AM - 10 PM or 12 midnight
Brunch: Sat & Sun: 9 AM - 5 PM

💳 $ **Entertainment:**
Fulton Street, the view

Cafe Fledermaus is a sandwich shop and ice cream parlor that tries to bill itself as a European cafe. It's unconvincing in the European department, but as a casual sandwich and dessert cafe they do pretty well. The inside looks like an ice cream parlor with a black-and-white checked floor and little round tables. The best place to sit is outside on the high stools around the tall round tables shaded by green umbrellas. Here you can have a nice lunch or light dinner complete with a fabulous dessert without breaking the bank. Options include clam chowder, salads, sandwiches, quiche, and pasta, including seafood varieties. Milk, fresh juices, lemonade, sodas, a range of European coffees, assorted beer, wine and a full bar are available. The big selection of desserts includes ice creams, cheesecakes, and Continental specialties such as strudel, Linzer torte, tiramisu, cannoli, and eclairs.

SOUTH STREET SEAPORT MUSEUM

Visitor's Center: 12 Fulton St.
(between South and Ferry Sts.)
(669-9400

Hours:

April 1 - Sept. 30:
10 AM - 6 PM; open Thu until 8 PM

Oct. 1 - March 31:
Wed-Mon: 10 AM - 5 PM; closed Tue

Admission:

Adults - $6; Seniors - $5;
Students - $4; Children - $3

Tickets can be purchased at the Visitor's Center, the Pier 16 ticket booth, and at the museum galleries.

Across Fulton Street from the fish market is a block of historic early nineteenth-century buildings called Schermerhorn Row, which houses the South Street Seaport Museum's Visitor's Center. Here you can obtain information about the many exhibitions, activities, and events presented by the museum at various sites. These include a children's center (165 John St.), a working re-creation of a nineteenth-century printing press (211 Water St.), and a maritime craft center and three galleries (171 John St., 209 & 213 Water Sts.) that house exhibitions such as *Immigration in the Age of Sail* and displays of model boats. The museum has an archeological dig site at 17 State Street called *New York Unearthed*. Kids can also "raise the sheets" during the two-hour-long public sails on the museum's schooner *Pioneer*, which departs daily (summer only, weather permitting) at 12:30, 3:30, 7, and 9 PM. Tickets are $16 for adults and $6 for kids under 12. Reservations are suggested (669-9400).

STATUE OF LIBERTY ELLIS ISLAND

• •

Two American treasures, both managed by the National Park Service, are within easy reach of New York City and make for a great family day trip for less than the cost of going to the movies. Ferries to the Statue of Liberty and Ellis Island run approximately every 30 minutes every day of the year except Christmas, from 9:15 AM until around 5 PM. Leaving from Battery Park at the southern tip of Manhattan, the ferries first travel to Liberty Island (15 to 20 minutes' sailing time), then to Ellis Island (approximately ten more minutes), then back to Battery Park (about 15 minutes). While there is a charge for ferry tickets, admission to both national parks is free. Tickets for same-day travel can be purchased at the ticket office at the Castle Clinton National Monument, itself a historic fort that once defended the New York Harbor and, prior to 1892, processed more than seven million people emigrating to America. The lines both for the ticket office and to board the ferry can be very long (especially in the summer and on weekends), so go as early as possible. If you *do* get stuck in line and the kids get hungry, there are pushcart vendors who sell sodas, ice cream, pretzels, and hot dogs. Once on board the ferry, there is a snack bar that sells hot dogs, chips, soft vanilla ice cream, candy, cake, sodas, and hot chocolate.

BATTERY PARK/CASTLE CLINTON

☏ 269-5755

🚇 1,9 to South Ferry
(exit is from the first five cars only)

Ferry Tickets:
Adults: $7; Kids over 3 yrs. old: $3; Seniors: $5

STATUE OF LIBERTY NATIONAL MONUMENT

Free

(363-7620

The Statue of Liberty, which is clearly the more popular of the two destinations, has been open as a park since 1886. The neoclassical statue was designed by the French sculptor Frédéric-Auguste Bartholdi and is formally titled *Liberty Enlightening the World*. It was conceived by the statesman Edouard de Laboulaye in 1865 to commemorate the French and American alliance during the American Revolution. Although funding and construction delays did not allow the full statue to be unveiled until October 1886, Liberty's raised arm and torch were completed in time for the International Centennial (of American Independence) Exhibition in Philadelphia in 1876.

The copper and steel statue, a gift from the people of France, weighs 225 tons and is 151 feet high. The 85 foot granite pedestal was designed by Richard Morris Hunt. Funding for the pedestal and the 65 foot concrete base came from many small donations by American individuals and was organized by Joseph Pulitzer. At the time of its dedication, the Statue of Liberty was the tallest structure in New York.

Bartholdi selected Bedloe's Island (the name was changed to Liberty Island in 1956) as the site for the statue so that the first view of the New World for millions of travelers and immigrants would be of Liberty welcoming them to America. The entire statue was built in France and shipped to New York in crates.

The interior support structure was designed by Alexandre-Gustave Eiffel, who later designed the famed Eiffel Tower of Paris.

You can climb the 22 story staircase to the crown or take an elevator to the top of the pedestal, ten floors up. There is a museum on the second and third floors chronicling the building of the statue and immigration to America. If you intend to climb the staircase, go to the top of the pedestal, or visit the museum, you must take one of the very first ferries (no exaggeration) as there is only one line and by the 11 AM ferry, even on a summer weekday, the wait to get in will be several hours long. We usually just walk the promenade, picnic in the park, and enjoy the great views of Manhattan. There are many outdoor kiosks and pushcarts that sell ice cream and drinks, and a nice outdoor cafe with pretty metal tables and benches surrounded by planters full of flowers. The cafe is self-service and the food includes hot dogs, burgers, chicken or fish platters, fries, tuna salad, and fruit cup. Also sold are sodas, juice, water, coffee, tea, ice cream, and cookies. The prices are low — $2.50 for burgers, $1.50 for hot dogs — and the food is OK.

ELLIS ISLAND NATIONAL MONUMENT

Free
(363-7620

The next stop on the ferry ride is Ellis Island, which, abandoned in 1954, was reopened in 1990 after eight years of renovation at a cost of $156 million. The main building is now the Ellis Island

Immigration Museum and houses fascinating exhibits chronicling the stories of some of the more than 12 million immigrants processed here from 1892 until 1954. Starting with the baggage room exhibit, where there is actual luggage of immigrants on display, there are many exhibits that kids seven and older can relate to. You can follow the steps of the poor steerage passengers through the rooms where they were registered, examined, questioned, and eventually cleared to become residents of the New World. There is a great walking-tour tape, narrated by Tom Brokaw, that you can rent, or you can just wander through the museum. There are many moving photographs, easy-to-understand displays, and an excellent free film, *Island of Hopes, Island of Tears.*

Outside the museum is a park with great water views. Here, too, is the American Immigrant Wall of Honor, which lists more than 420,000 families. A new section of the wall will be built in 1998, and there is still room on it for additional names. If you are interested in honoring a relative or a friend, you can make arrangements at the Island (there is a mandatory donation) or by contacting the Ellis Island Foundation in New York.

There is an inexpensive self-service cafe that offers pizzas, burgers, salads, and sandwiches like tuna, ham and cheese, corned beef, and submarine. There are snacks available like muffins, bagels, nachos, and ice cream. Beverage options are the usual sodas, milk, OJ, hot chocolate, and beer. You can eat your food outside at the stone picnic tables, with magnificent views of both the Statue of Liberty and Manhattan. In addition, there are little snack carts that sell ice cream and beverages near the ferry waiting area.

WORLD FINANCIAL CENTER
WINTER GARDEN
BATTERY PARK CITY PARKS

WORLD FINANCIAL CENTER
∙∙

West St. (between Vesey and Liberty Sts. along Hudson River) across the West Side Highway from the World Trade Center

☎ General information: 945-0505
Open daily

TRANSPORTATION:

🚇 1,9 to Courtland St.;
A,E to Chambers St./World Trade Center

Walking from World Trade Center:
Follow signs, walk over pedestrian North Bridge to Winter Garden

Trans Hudson ferry:
Hoboken NJ Transit train station to & from WFC Jersey City/Colgate at Exchange Pl. to & from WFC
Hours:
Mon-Fri: 6:50 AM - 10:50 PM
(approx. every 10-20 minutes)
Sat & Sun: 10 AM - 9:50 PM
(approx. every 30 minutes)
Fare: $2 one way

Indoor Parking:
Kinney Parking: 1 hour: $10; 2-10 hrs.: $16.75
#1, 200 Albany St. (between West St. & South End Ave., 1 block south of Liberty St.) 768-9714
#4, North End Ave.
(along Hudson River off Vesey St.) 285-9842
Gateway Garage: 1 hour: $10; $1 ea. add'l hour
345 South End Ave. (at Gateway Plaza)
321-2316

WINTER GARDEN

••••••••••••••••••••••••••••••••••

(Arts & events information: 945-2600
Open daily
Gallery Store hours: Mon-Fri: 10 AM - 7 PM;
Sat: 11 AM - 6 PM; Sun 12 noon - 5 PM

The World Financial Center, Winter Garden, and especially the beautiful Battery Park City parks are terrific for families. The WFC/Winter Garden complex houses offices, a shopping center, and a public concert and exhibition space. Events staged in the dramatic five story glass-domed Winter Garden, with its 45-foot-tall palm trees, are generally free to the public on an open-seating basis. Live radiothon benefits, flower shows, culinary festivals, and concerts are examples of the types of events.

In the surrounding WFC/Winter Garden shopping gallery are some of the stores typically found in upscale suburban shopping malls, including Ann Taylor, Barneys, and Gap Kids clothing stores; Caswell-Massey toiletries; Godiva Chocolatier; and Rizzoli International Bookstore. A dozen or so restaurants are located at the WFC. Pipeline and Edward Moran Bar & Grill are our two favorites for family dining. Both are located on the WFC Plaza in the midst of the Battery Park City park system and have fabulous water views.

BATTERY PARK CITY PARKS

The Battery Park City park system comprises almost 30 acres of protected open public space. Extending from Battery Place at the southern tip of Manhattan along the Hudson River north to Chambers Street, the parks include large open meadows, playgrounds, manicured public gardens, and well-tended community gardens. The esplanade, with several public plazas, runs the length of the park system along the river. Sailing vessels and yachts dock in the cove harbors. The Trans Hudson Ferry terminal is conveniently located adjacent to the WFC Plaza.

Operated by the nonprofit Battery Park City Parks Corporation, the parks are maintained using only natural fertilizers and insect controls, no toxic chemicals. Notices are posted advising what is currently in bloom. Ample bench seating is provided, and the park system is accessible to the handicapped. The brick-paved plazas and esplanade are great for rollerblading, sunning, and strolling. We especially like the whimsical bronze sculptures of Tom Otterness. Look for his newest installation at the red gravel park located north of the WFC Plaza; it features elf construction workers and 'sounding ears'. Excellent family-oriented events such as play groups, family dancing lessons, fishing, and interactive music concerts are scheduled from May through October. Some events, like Drawing in the Park, require registration. Call 267-9700 for more information and a full schedule.

EDWARD MORAN BAR & GRILL

1 World Financial Center
(250 Vesey St. at WFC Plaza)

(945-2255

Hours:
Mon-Fri: 11:30 AM - 10 PM
Sat & Sun:11:30 AM - 6 or 8 PM
Brunch: Sat & Sun: All day

 $-$$ **Entertainment:** Coloring menu

Located near the fountain on the north side of the harbor plaza, Edward Moran Bar & Grill is a great place to eat outside in the sun on a beautiful day. (With kids, don't bother going inside; it's more formal, with a club atmosphere.) You can't go wrong with the half-pound burgers, although they're expensive at $10.95. Both Caesar and mesclun salads are served, as is a nice onion soup with Fontina cheese. For a light meal, you might want to try the grilled vegetables with mozzarella and balsamic vinegar or the skewered chicken and peppers with ginger soy sauce. The menu also includes $13 to $16 entrees, but we have never gone here for a serious sit-down dinner.

The well-priced kid's menu ($2-3) offers PB&J, fruit salad, grilled cheese, macaroni and cheese, hot dogs, and burgers. It also is an acitvity sheet with word games, a maze and a scene to color. We also suggest a stop here for refreshments and dessert. It's a great place to relax and people/harbor watch while enjoying apple pie à la mode, carrot cake, or ice cream sundaes with chocolate chip cookies.

PIPELINE
2 World Financial Center
(225 Liberty St. at WFC Plaza)

(945-2755
<u>**Hours:**</u>
Mon-Wed: 11 AM - 9 PM
Thu & Fri: 11 AM - 10 PM
Sat & Sun: 11 AM - 8 PM
Brunch: Sat & Sun: 11 AM - 5 PM

 $-$$ **Entertainment:** Yes

Attracting a business lunch crowd during the week, Pipeline is all families at other times, especially summer weekends. One of the two restaurants at the WFC Plaza that we recommend for families, it's a good place to enjoy a basic meal while listening to the waves and boat horns. Since it is right on the water, you can sit outside and watch your kids if they want to play on the plaza. Inside, Pipeline is designed to resemble an oil refinery with concrete walls, brightly colored pipes, and ladders. The Saturday and Sunday night children's movies attract a local crowd in the winter. Tables are pushed aside in the main dining room to make room for beanbag chairs and a large rug, so kids can be comfortable while they watch the animated videos on a large screen.

The kids' menu doubles as a clown mask. It offers pancakes, nachos, grilled cheese, tuna sandwiches, chicken fingers, pasta, dogs and burgers. These are priced at $4.25 to $6.25 with a drink and dessert. The main menu is standard American fare, with soups and salads, sandwiches, burgers, pastas, and grilled entrees. In addition to sodas, juice, and milk, they make shakes and egg creams, and have a full bar. Service can be slow... don't come here if you are in a rush. And we suggest you stick with the basic items. The burgers are very popular, the fish sandwich is excellent, and the soups are pretty good. Menu prices are about $5 higher than they should be, so relax and enjoy the view — you're paying for it.

WORLD TRADE CENTER OBSERVATORIES

2 World Trade Center
Church Street (between Vesey and Liberty Sts.)
(General information: 435-4170
(Observatories information: 323-2340

🚇 1,9 to Courtland St.;
   A,E to Chambers St.- World Trade Center

OBSERVATORIES
Hours: 9:30 AM - 9:30 PM
Ticket office is on the Plaza level.
Admission: Adults - $10; Seniors - $8;
Kids 6 to 12 - $5; Kids under 6 - Free
Note: Price includes helicopter simulation ride.
After ticket purchase and security inspection, you will be directed to the observatory elevators.

TKTS OFFICE: Two World Trade Center, Plaza level (Downtown branch of tkts, off-price Broadway ticket sales.)
Hours: Mon-Fri: 11 AM - 5 PM; Sat: 11 AM - 3 PM

The World Trade Center is a five-building complex and plaza located on five acres bordered by Church, Vesey, Liberty, and West Streets. Completed in the 1970s, its construction created sufficient landfill to provide over 20 acres of Battery Park. Having recently reopened after a multimillion-dollar facelift, the observation decks of the World Trade Center now offer visitors a mini New York theme park and breathtaking bird's-eye views of the city, Long Island, the Statue of Liberty, and New Jersey. Located on the 107th and 110th floors of 2 World Trade Center, one of the famous twin towers, the observatories are open daily from 9:30 AM. Try to arrive as early as possible — the wait to go up is usually an hour long by 11 AM.

"Less than one minute from earth to heaven," our elevator operator explained as we whooshed up the 1,300 feet to the 107th floor. The observation deck on this level is glass-enclosed, a well-appreci-ated fact on a cold or windy day. White metal benches set at the very edge of the windowed perimeter allowed us to look directly down. Sam and his pals enjoyed pointing out the numbers on the roofs of buses, the tops of people's heads, and the structures on buildings far below. Video infor-mation monitors provide multi-lingual descrip-tions of all the major visible landmarks. Digital transmitting kiosks allow kids to send cus-tomized "Messages to the Stars."

Created by a designer who has worked on many Disney attractions, the center area has been ren-ovated with a fantasy quality that kids love. It's a lot of fun to follow the kinetic moving ball sculp-ture over and around the incredible 50-building scale model of Manhattan. There are two gift shops, and a New York style food court modeled after a subway car. A six minute motion-simulat-ed helicopter tour of Manhattan can be viewed at no additional cost.

Up a couple of escalators, the open-air 110th floor observation deck is truly the "Top of the World." It is an amazing experience to take in these sweep-ing urban vistas from 1,366 feet up with no roof over your head. Be sure to bring quarters for the telescopes. And if you are there in the evening, you can catch the rooftop light show, which is also vis-ible from the ground.

Family dining options in this part of downtown are limited and difficult. If the kids are hungry, your best bet is the 107th-floor food court. It offers food considered New York in character, fast food in quality, at slightly inflated prices. The grill cooks up hot dogs, knishes, ribs, French fries, and onion rings. A S'barro franchise sells pizza, pastas, chicken parmesan, and salads. The gourmet coffee kiosk also has milk, juice, cheesecake, and cookies. Off to the side of a seating area loosely modeled on Central Park are popcorn, pretzel, and cotton candy pushcart vendors. Look around — there may even be an ice cream man.

Another option is to have a snack here and walk across the North Bridge to the World Financial Center Plaza restaurants. For more information, see the WFC review.

SOHO and NOHO

SoHo, the area south of Houston Street (hence the name), is bounded by Canal Street to the south, Washington Street to the west and the Bowery to the east. It is also defined by its many art galleries and trendy shops and restaurants.

NoHo extends north from Houston Street (hence its name), to East 8th Street/Astor Place and from Mercer Street on the west to the Bowery. This area includes Cooper Square and a part of Broadway heavily populated by NYU students.

RESTAURANTS

CUPPING ROOM CAFE

359 West Broadway
(between Broome & Grand Sts.)

☏ 925-2898

🚇 A,C,E to Canal St.; N,R to
Prince St.; 6 to Spring St.

Hours:

Breakfast/Lunch:
Mon-Fri: 7:30 AM - 5 PM

Dinner:
Mon-Fri: 6 PM - 1 AM
Sat: 6 PM - 2 AM
Sun: 6 PM - 12 midnight

Brunch: Sat & Sun: 8 AM - 5 PM

💳 $$-$$$ **Entertainment:**
Live jazz Fri & Sat at 9 PM

Note: Reservations accepted for Mon-Fri only

From the street, the Cupping Room Cafe looks like yet another SoHo bar, but the cool, simple elegance inside is a nice surprise. The medium-sized dining room, sandwiched between two antique wooden bars, has old bistro-type lamps hanging from the high tin ceiling, and exposed brick and ochre-colored walls displaying large color photographs of doors, windows, and chairs. The tables and deep armchairs are appropriately spaced, and oversized bouquets of flowers and recordings of old jazz vocalists complete the ambiance.

Perfect for a special occasion or for when the grandparents are along, meals are least expensive on Tuesday nights when a $13.95 prix-fixe dinner is offered. Otherwise, try the weekend brunch. Though not necessary for an early dinner, reservations are accepted during the week and are probably a good idea. The service here is excellent, and they go out of their way to make your child feel like royalty.

The new American-style food is well prepared and the portions are generous. Kids can select from pasta, chicken, strip steak, lamb chops, and the fish of the day, which can be grilled, blackened, or poached. There are grilled cheese sandwiches and an absolutely fabulous grilled sirloin burger with homemade fries. In addition to a large selection of salads (we suggest the watercress and endive, served with goat cheese, walnuts and a roasted-beet vinaigrette, or the smoked salmon Caesar); there are also vegetarian dishes such as stir fry over rice. Drinks include hot white chocolate, sodas, juice (including freshly squeezed OJ), milk, coffee, tea, and a full bar with a nice (but expensive) wine list. Topping it all off are the tempting homemade desserts.

IL CORALLO TRATTORIA

176 Prince St. (between Thompson & Sullivan Sts.)

📞 941-7119

🚇 C,E to Spring St.

Hours:
12 noon - 12 midnight
Brunch:
Sat & Sun: 12 noon - 4 PM

💳 **$-$$**   **Entertainment:** No

We first noticed Il Corallo one summer evening while walking in SoHo after dinner. Most of the restaurants we passed were empty, but Il Corallo was packed, with a long line of people waiting to get in. One of the mothers waiting for a table told us her family came to eat there because the kids liked the pizza and the adults thought their low-priced pasta dishes were terrific.

We went back the next night and our meal proved her right. The restaurant is small — it can handle around 60 to 75 diners at its plain wood-trimmed tables. There is a simple Mediterranean feel to the room — the floor is red tile, and the vanilla-colored walls are sparsely decorated with old maps, a wreath of dried red peppers, and a wooden sculpture of a fish. In season, the bifold window/doors open, allowing the restaurant to spill out into a sidewalk cafe. The conversation level (which may include as much Italian and French as English) is such that the kids can get a little loud without disturbing someone else's meal, but as the tables are small and quite close, children under six might be out of place here after 7 PM (when the restaurant gets crowded).

There are 15 to 20 salad and antipasto choices, depending on the daily specials, all priced between $3.50 and $5.95 and all large enough to be a meal in themselves. We adults always order the bocconcini — fresh mozzarella balls layered on top of tomatoes, prosciutto, roasted peppers, sundried tomatoes and Parmesan. Other starters worth checking out are the antipasto di campo (a salad of greens, asparagus, peppers, Parmesan, and prosciutto) and the grilled vegetables.

Sam and friends almost always order the delicious crispy thin-crust pizza. The main reason to come here, however, is the pasta. The 50-plus dishes, all under $10, include taglierini Sorrento (black squid ink linguine with lobster, shrimp, clams, and scallops in a tomato sauce), goat cheese ravioli, and fettuccine Molisane (green noodles with chicken and sundried tomatoes in a cream sauce). Daily specials include meat, chicken, and fish, including sautéed red snapper. Weekdays until 4 PM there is a $7.95 lunch special of soup or salad and a choice of pizza, pasta, gourmet sandwiches, grilled chicken, or a plate of mozzarella, prosciutto and tomato on mesclun. Beverage choices are milk, soda, coffee, beer, and wine from a good-sized list. They also have classic Italian desserts, but Sam and his friends found them too "fancy."

Although the staff is congenial and well-intentioned, the service on one visit was disorganized and we made repeated requests for items. The pluses outweigh this minus, however, so this hasn't stopped us from returning.

KELLEY and PING

127 Greene St. (between Houston & Prince Sts.)

☎ 228-1212

🚇 N,R to Prince St.; B,D,F,Q to Broadway/Lafayette St.

Hours:
Lunch: 11:30 AM - 5 PM
Dinner: 6 - 11 PM
Brunch: No

$$ **Entertainment:** No

This Asian grocery store and noodle shop occupies a long and narrow former industrial space and reminds us of what the rest of SoHo looked like 20 years ago. Bare light bulbs hang from the painted tin ceiling, and the old wooden factory floor and whitewashed brick walls give a bohemian character. Where else can you eat where the walls are decorated with bottles of soy sauce and vinegar, hanging woks, and bags of rice (all of which you can purchase)? The multinational Asian food is cooked in a kitchen set in the middle of the dining area, visible to all.

Because of its tasty, well-priced food, Kelley and Ping has developed a real neighborhood following that includes families with children. Kids usually like the chicken satay grilled on wooden skewers and the steamed vegetable or shrimp dumplings (both $5.50). We have also had success with nau yang (grilled sirloin, $14.95), grilled Vietnamese pork chops ($10.95), and sliced lemongrass chicken ($10.25), all of which are served with a delicious lemongrass, soy and garlic

BBQ sauce. Another great chicken dish is the kai kolae, a chicken breast braised in coconut milk and served sliced on shredded lettuce with a terrific coconut and red curry sauce. For children, we recommend that you request the meals with all the side dishes and sauces on a separate plate — some can be quite spicy.

Be sure to try some of the starters. The Vietnamese ravioli ($6.25) is a soft, flat steamed rice noodle that is rolled up like a tortilla and filled with chopped chicken, shitake mushrooms, lemongrass, and cilantro. Hae kun ($6.50) is mashed shrimp, chicken, and scallions deep-fried in a crispy tofu wrapper, and served with a spicy duck sauce. Other dishes range from Toyko noodles (shrimp and vegetable tempura with soba noodles in broth), to stir-fry items such as Chinese broccoli with ginger and oyster sauce, and salads with soy sesame dressing.

Besides milk, juice and sodas, there are wines, including sake and plum wine, and beers from China, Japan, Thailand and Holland. The desserts here are well worth the calories. The fried bananas wrapped in a spring roll with ice cream and ginger sauce are out of this world. The round brownie is thick and fudgy without being too sweet, and the restaurant serves Oriental ice cream flavors — green tea, coconut, red bean, and ginger.

LOMBARDI'S

32 Spring St. (between Mott & Mulberry Sts.)

(941-7994

🚇 6 to Spring St.

Hours:
Mon-Thu: 11:30 AM - 11 PM
Fri & Sat:
11:30 AM - 12 midnight
Sun: 11:30 AM - 10 PM
Brunch: No

🚭 $ **Entertainment:** Watching pizza chefs

In 1897, Gennaro Lombardi came to America and started making pizza. In 1905 he opened the first pizzeria in America, making pizzas as his father and his grandfather, both bakers back in Naples, had taught him. They have a delicious, homemade sauce, first-quality cheese and toppings, a crust which is a little thicker than *John's*, and it folds easily without cracking. In fact, John Sasso of *John's* and Anthony Pero of *Totonno's* both studied and worked at Lombardi's before opening their own pizzerias.

The original Lombardi's operated from 1905 until 1987. Gennaro Lombardi's grandson opened the current Lombardi's in 1994 across the street from the original location. Here the pizza is made as the Lombardis have always made it, in a small restaurant with Old World ambiance not to be found in tacky tourist imitations.

The menu is simple and basic — two sizes of pizzas with a choice of 14 toppings like sweet Italian sausages, roasted red peppers, wild mushrooms, and Calamata olives. There's also a white pizza made with three cheeses (fresh mozzarella, ricotta, and pecorino romano), garlic, and no sauce, as well as fresh clam pie, calzones, and a large house mesclun salad. Milk, sodas, coffee, and a small wine list are offered. Everything is reasonably priced; the service is engaging in a neighborhood way and very fast.

The restaurant is casual. Red and white tablecloths under glass adorn the small tables and vinyl booths. On one wall, faded Neapolitan murals are painted directly on the exposed bricks. Old photographs of pizza making and the first restaurant decorate others. The painted tin ceiling has fans, and the floor is laid with small hexagonal tiles. There are two long narrow front dining rooms and an upstairs back deck where the food is served picnic style (i.e. paper plates and cups).

Sam's favorite places are the tables in the small dining room across from the pizza chefs, who love kids and are very friendly. They take the time to show kids the art of making and baking pizzas. They have even let Sam make his own miniature pizza, then baked it for him.

NOHO STAR

330 Lafayette St. (at Bleecker St.)

☏ 925-0070

🚇 6 to Bleecker St.;
N,R to Prince St.; B,D,Q,F to
Broadway/Lafayette St.

Hours:
Breakfast: Mon-Fri: 8 - 11:30 AM
Lunch: 11:30 AM - 4:30 PM
Dinner: 4:30 PM - 12 midnight

Brunch:
Sat & Sun: 10:30 AM - 4:30 PM

▬ $$ **Entertainment:** No

Note: Outdoor cafe in warmer weather.

The sense of well being that's pervasive at the NoHo Star can be attributed to a lot of little details taken together, rather than to any one element: the floor-to-ceiling windows that seem to bring in the street, yet keep the room inside protected and private; the fun decor that includes squiggly painted beams and yellow polka-dotted bathroom walls; the jazz and swing music on the stereo; the energetic conversations; the occasional rumble of the subway. One thing is sure — the food, prepared in an open white-tiled kitchen with a beautiful copper ceiling — can be remarkable.

Sometimes it feels like family night here. Looking around at the other diners seated in the rattan chairs at their wood and marble tables, you'll find kids from infants to teens eating with their parents. Of course a wide range of adults living in this artists' neighborhood of NoHo also eat here.

(We have been told that the "Star" in the restaurant's name honors the newspaper that occupied this space.)

The cuisine is New American with a Chinese flair. The menu is interesting and wide-ranging, offering spaghettini with shrimp and green fennel pesto, roasted salmon with black bean sauce, Peking duck salad with warm vinaigrette, Buddha's vegetable feast for the minor gods, and Szechuan beef with carrots, scallions, and celery. The owner (a former doctor at St. Vincent's Hospital), owns several other restaurants including Elephant & Castle (see review) and a Chinese restaurant in San Francisco. A full Chinese dinner menu is available daily from 6 PM. And while Sam prefers to order the burgers here (which are first quality) with a side order of fries (among his favorite), other good kid choices are pasta, grilled chicken breast, tuna and swordfish steaks.

Beverages include sodas, freshly made ginger ale, milk and a full bar. If you wish, you can bring your own wine. A number of chocolate temptations are offered for dessert, including Murder by Chocolate, Heart of Darkness, and hot fudge sundaes; crème brûlée, banana splits, carrot cake, and sherbets are on the menu as well. Waiters are intelligent, well informed, and efficient.

So if you are looking for an upbeat, lighthearted place to dine on some seriously good food, try the NoHo Star. We think that this restaurant represents some of what living in New York City is all about, and we have friends who love this place so much that they don't think twice about dining here two nights in a row.

SILVER SPURS

490 La Guardia Pl. (at Houston St.)

☎ 228-2333
🚆 1,9 to Houston St.

Hours:
Breakfast: 7 - 11 AM
Lunch/Dinner:
Sun-Thu: 11 AM - 12 midnight
Fri & Sat: 11 AM - 2 AM
Brunch: No

💳 $ **Entertainment:** No

You can't miss the large bright sign outside this new, upscale version of the Greenwich Village institution. It simply says "GRUB" and with a telephone number like 228-BEEF, you don't have to be a genius to figure out what the fare is. While we wouldn't go out of our way to take kids to the original location, the SoHo outpost is attractive, especially for a place that serves 20 types of ten-ounce burgers, ranging in price from $3.95 (the basic) to $9.95 (with bacon, ham, cheese, mushrooms, tomatoes, onions, and fries).

The restaurant has an attractive silvery decor, from the oversized ceiling fans that look as if they belong on the front of an airplane to aluminum chairs with bright blue vinyl seats. Colorful light fixtures provide nice accents. There is a small bar in the back and the adjacent kitchen is open to view from the street.

The menu is much like a Greek coffee shop's. Besides burgers, you'll find the usual salads, bar-type appetizers, soups, omelets, sandwiches that range from basic to gourmet, po'boys, and nine different chicken combos. If that's not enough, there are $7 to $14 entrees, including fish and steak. Sodas, juice, milk, shakes and coffee (plus alcohol) are beverage options, and desserts include ice creams, cakes, and pies. Prices are low, especially for SoHo (technically this restaurant is on the Village side of Houston St.), service is competent, and the kitchen will make up specials for kids.

Note: Greenwich Village location (See review): 771 Broadway (at E. 9th St.) 473-5517/8.

SOHO KITCHEN & BAR

103 Greene St. (between Prince & Spring Sts.)

☎ 925-1866

🚇 6 to Spring St.; N,R to Prince

Hours:
Mon-Thu: 11:30 AM - 11:45 PM
Fri & Sat: 11:30 AM - 2 AM
Sun: 12 noon - 9:45 PM
Brunch: Sun: 12 noon - 4 PM

💳 $$ **Entertainment:** No

 6+

Wheelchair Access: Call ahead for assistance

Finding a trendy restaurant in SoHo is simple, but finding one that's friendly to kids can be a bit trickier. SoHo Kitchen and Bar is one of those rare places in that neighborhood that welcome kids. Moreover, the food is great and the atmosphere is casual and relaxed. This expansive renovated warehouse is dramatic, with 20-foot-high brick walls, huge modern paintings, and tables set into alcoves or along banquettes.

KIDS EAT NEW YORK

While the menu does not feature specific children's specials, their ten-inch pizzas ($8.75 to $10.75) are a good size for one child, and the kitchen makes an excellent burger (beef, turkey or chicken, all for around $7). Roast beef, chicken, smoked turkey, proscuitto and smoked salmon sandwiches are served. Beverages include milk, sodas, and juice, and for dessert there are brownies, apple pie, and ice cream.

The regular menu is the bar type – chicken wings, chili, salads, and pastas, plus a few Middle Eastern items such as hummus and tabbouleh. However, we suggest you order one of the daily "specials," which are usually outstanding. Try the port-marinated grilled flank steak, served with a corn medley and mashed potatoes, the chicken paillard, and pasta specials such as the fusilli with chicken, mushrooms, and vegetables. The restaurant is well-known for its wine list, all available by the glass or in "flights" — 1-1/2 ounce tastings of three to seven different wines presented by classification. Seven-ounce beer "flights" are also offered. The flight theme is echoed in SoHo Kitchen's decor — enormous model airplanes and mallard ducks soar from the ceiling above the handsome central bar.

TENNESSEE MOUNTAIN

143 Spring St. (at Wooster St.)

☎ 431-3993

🚇 N,R to Prince St.,
E,C,6 to Spring St.

Hours:
Lunch: Mon-Fri: 11:30 AM - 4 PM
Dinner:
Mon-Wed: 4 - 11 PM
Thu-Sat: 4 PM- 12 midnight
Sun: 4 - 10 PM

Brunch:
Sat & Sun: 11:30 AM - 3:30 PM

 $$ **Entertainment:** No

Note: Not suitable for young children after 8 PM on Friday & Saturday nights as restaurant can get a little rowdy.

Tennessee Mountain is a rustic surprise tucked away in SoHo, the half of the restaurant that faces Spring Street being a landmark farmhouse dating from 1807. Its Monday night all-you-can-eat-and-drink special ($16.95) is only one of the reasons to come here.

If you are a vegetarian, this is not the place for you. This restaurant is all about BBQ — steaks, chicken, ribs, and burgers, plus all the fixings like corn on the cob, baked beans, and mashed potatoes. The baby back ribs are out of this world, and the kitchen also does a nice job with grilled fish and shrimp. Ask for the kids' menu, which offers burgers, chicken fingers, chicken franks, grilled cheese, and PB&J, all with fries, for $3.95 to $4.95. In addition to milk, soda, and apple mash in season, there is a full bar.

The restaurant itself is simple and clean. The open grill on the first floor is also visible from the balcony of one of the two upstairs dining rooms, which we prefer. The walls are lined with old photographs and maps of New York and Tennessee, and the worn wood floors complement the charcoal smells that waft from the grill. Green factory lamps hang over the wooden tables and booths. There is also a second-floor outdoor cafe. The restaurant has a nice, casual ambiance and unlike many of the neighboring "sophisticated" European-style restaurants, Tennessee Mountain welcomes kids.

TIME CAFE

380 Lafayette St.
(between Great Jones St. & E. 4th St.)

☎ 533-7000

🚇 6 to Astor Place;
N,R to 8th St./NYU

Hours:
Self-serve Breakfast:
Mon-Fri: 8 - 11:30 AM
Lunch: Mon-Fri: 12 noon - 4 PM
Daily Light Fare Menu: 4 - 6 PM
Dinner:
Sun-Thu: 6 PM - 12 midnight
Fri & Sat: 6 PM - 1 AM

Brunch:
Sat & Sun: 10:30 AM - 4 PM

💳 $$

Entertainment: Crayons, coloring books, postcards, kids' magazines.

Sam likes the the big clock over the bar whose hands rapidly move backward, one of the wacky decorative features here. The restaurant is large and airy, with very high ceilings, huge windows, and a good amount of "stroller-friendly" space between tables. Bring the family here if it's not too late (otherwise there will be a wait).

Kid choices include six different personal-sized pizzas, a half dozen types of pasta, ten-ounce burgers, and grilled or BBQ free-range chicken served in several different ways. The daily home-made soups (such as the carrot rosemary) and the gazpacho are quite popular with adults, as are the black bean and cheese quesadillas and the smoked Scottish salmon rolls with avocado. Other favorite entrees are the sesame-crusted salmon with wasabi and the large market salad that includes tabbouleh, lentils, goat cheese and an assortment of grilled vegetables. Drinks are the standard sodas and milk; there is a full bar and wine list. You won't have to worry about the kids being a little noisy or wandering about, as every-one here takes it in stride. There are coloring books and crayons, but you may have to ask the waiter for them.

GREENWICH VILLAGE

• •

The quaint section known as the **West Village** is the area from 14th Street on the north to Houston Street on the south, the Hudson River to the west and Seventh Avenue to the east.

The center of the Village, which we refer to as **Greenwich Village**, is also bordered by 14th Street and Houston Street and extends from Seventh Avenue to Broadway.

The funky **East Village** goes from Broadway to the East River and from Houston Street to 14th Street.

RESTAURANTS

....

ANGLERS & WRITERS

420 Hudson St. (at St. Luke's Pl.)

📞 675-0810

🚇 1,9 to Houston St.;
A,B,C,D,E,F,Q to W. 4th St.

<u>**Hours:**</u>
Breakfast: Mon-Fri: 9 - 11:30 AM
High Tea: 3 - 7 PM
Lunch/Dinner:
Mon-Thu: 11:30 AM - 11 PM
Fri & Sat: 11:30 AM - 12 midnight
Sun: 11:30 AM - 10 PM
Brunch: (No reservations)
Sat: 9 AM - 4 PM;
Sun: 10 AM - 4 PM

$$ **Entertainment:** No

Note: Wheelchair accessible but up one step.

Located on the site of an ancient trout stream, this wonderful restaurant appears to be right out of *A River Runs Through It*. It's decorated with old oil paintings of the ones that didn't get away, as well as all sorts of angling paraphernalia — tackle boxes, campfire pans, wicker creels and fishing rods and reels.

As we are seated at one of the large oak tables (dressed up with a crocheted doily and mason jar of wildflowers), the maitre d' delights the children with an impromptu lesson on how to "pitch" trading cards. Kids will like just about everything on the American home-cooking menu. Family-style dinners include a deep chicken potpie, lamb stew, and turkey casserole. You can order baked Bourbon-glazed ham, roasted chicken, an open-face turkey sandwich with gravy and dressing, and a selection of fresh fish. On the lighter side, try the tuna salad nicoise — a big bowl of endive, radicchio, and other lettuces, filled with olives, boiled eggs, and vegetables, covered with a light, creamy dressing. The hearty country food served here is fresh, filling, but never heavy.

For "high tea" we suggest you order the platter of open-faced Danish tea sandwiches. The weekend brunch is so popular that the line often stretches down the block. And the desserts, baked by the owner's mother, are heavenly. The list of pies and cakes changes daily (there is also ice cream for the kids), but every one of them that we have sampled tastes as good as our best memories of a favorite aunt's holiday baking.

Next door is The Bespeckled Trout, a quaint general store presided over by Anna, a local Italian grandmother. It's full of wares as varied as antique fishing lures and antique china teapots, all displayed on vintage glass-paned bins filled with old-fashioned candy — special treats for kids who have been good!

BAYAMO

704 Broadway
(between 4th St. & Washington Pl.)

☎ 475-5151
🚇 6 to Astor Pl., N,R to 8 St.

Hours:
Sun-Thu: 12 noon - 12 midnight
Fri & Sat: 12 noon - 1 AM
Brunch: (daily) 12 noon - 3 PM,
and 10 PM - 12 midnight

▬ $-$$ **Entertainment:** No

Are your kids fascinated with dragons? If so, check out Bayamo, a large, fun, and very casual restaurant with a Cuban/Chinese/American menu. Our favorite place to sit in the two-floor dining area is the well-lit balcony, where kids can wander about and amuse themselves with the cartoon-like sculpted decor.

Hanging over the bar is a large red Chinese junk that on further inspection turns out to be a giant chili pepper with chopsticks for oars. (Can you find the boat's prisoner?) Look over the door for the hand of the evil genie, complete with very long fingernails and exotic rings. And what are his chopsticks lifting? The body of a most unlucky … what? Speaking of luck, Sam reminded me that dragons are Chinese symbols of good luck. Remember that when you notice the enormous green bearded fellow who seems to have just broken through the back wall.

The staff is helpful in guiding one through the large eclectic menu. Kid-friendly choices include chicken fingers, pizza, quesadillas, and pasta. The burgers, steaks, and chicken grilled over lava rocks are very popular. For a more Oriental flavor, try the steamed or fried dumplings. Both the Cuban popcorn (fried crawfish tails) and the chorizo cheese raclette with guacamole are reorders for us. We loved the grilled shrimp portion of our brochette, but the swordfish was dark and fishy. And if you want to try a traditional Cuban dish, the ropa vieja is a braised shredded beef stew with plantains, yucca, beans, and rice.

BENDIX DINER
167 1st Ave. (between 10th & 11th Sts.)

☎ 260-4220

🚇 L to 14th St./1st Ave.;
6 to Astor Pl.

Hours:
Mon-Fri: 8 AM - 11 PM
Sat & Sun: 10 AM - 12 PM
Brunch:
Sat & Sun: 10 AM - 4 PM

 $-$$ **Entertainment:** No

Note: Candy treats for well-behaved kids

Replacing the Lucky Dog Diner, the Bendix Diner has come to the East Village, bringing both the family friendliness and the Thai/American menu of the Chelsea original. The decor is part art gallery and part funky East Village with Thai statuettes, strings of small lit hearts, and moving light designs projected on the ceiling.

81

KIDS EAT NEW YORK

When asked why the Bendix Diner is his favorite restaurant, our ten-year-old friend Leigh put it succinctly: "Because they have everything I want to eat." The menu is American diner with a dash of Thai. This unusual combination allows the kids to have burgers, fries, and a shake, while adults munch on pad Thai, Yaki soba (stir fried soba noodles with chicken and vegetables), or gai tom ka — coconut milk soup flavored with lemongrass. Kids usually like the Thai-style chicken satay (chicken barbecued on a wooden skewer) or the wontons (steamed or fried), as well as sandwich standbys such as grilled cheese, turkey, steak, chicken and tuna melts. Breakfast, available anytime, includes bagels and lox, eggs, granola, and stacks of fruit-filled buckwheat pancakes that are quite a challenge to finish.

In addition to the Chelsea menu (see Bendix Diner, Chelsea review), this location offers wine and 21 types of beer and ale, including brands from Brooklyn to Bangkok. You might also want to try the Hudson Valley farmhouse cider, the sparkling apple juice, and the unusual sodas made from guavas, pineapples, mandarins, or fruit punch. And kids, here's a tip: The waiter has a free after-dinner surprise, so be good!

Chelsea location:
219-221 8th Ave.
(at 21st St.) 366-0560

BUS STOP COFFEE SHOP

597 Hudson St. (Abingdon Sq. at Bethune St.)

☎ 206-1100

🚇 A,C,E,L, 1,2,3 to 14th St.

Hours:

6 AM - 10:45 PM

Brunch: Breakfast available daily all day long

 $ **Entertainment:** No

This cute little corner restaurant is named after a bus stop where many drivers take a break in between runs. With its white walls, tin ceiling, and simple flower arrangements adorning the tables, this is a nice, clean, inexpensive place for a simple family meal. The restaurant is very small — there are only nine little booths and four little tables — but the service is fast and friendly. We like to sit at one of the booths next to the windows.

The menu is standard American fare — burgers, salads, soups, and a wide range of sandwiches. In addition to the specials of the day, which are a good buy, there are pork chops, chicken, turkey, sirloin steak, or fish. Dessert is ice cream or the daily special. Besides sodas, kids can order milk, hot chocolate or shakes. There is also an assortment of coffees, teas, wine, and beer.

COWGIRL HALL OF FAME
519 Hudson St. (at 10th St.)

☎ 633-1133

🚇 1,9 to Christopher St.

Hours:
Lunch: Mon-Fri: 12 noon- 4 PM
Dinner:
Sun-Thu: 5 - 11:30 PM
Fri & Sat: 5 PM - 12:30 AM
Brunch:
Sat & Sun: 11:30 AM - 4 PM

💳 AMEX only **$-$$**   **Entertainment:** No

Whenever I suggest that we eat at Cowgirl's, Sam lets out a YEE - HAA! He thinks that it is one of the most fun restaurants around, and a lot of other kids agree. Everyone welcomes children here, it's OK to be noisy and you can wander around a bit. Cowgirl's western theme has a kitschy Greenwich Village twist. The checkered table-cloths, antler chandeliers, and skull and cactus decor, which adults may feel is over the top, makes for a perfect dining room for kids. We have always been seated right away, but that may be because we generally eat earlier than the older crowd.

The front of the restaurant is a general store that carries all sorts of stuff, from rabbit-foot key rings to fringed vests and penny candy. But this is not the only diversion available — the walls are loaded with western memorabilia that's lots of fun to look at.

The service here has always been pretty good. The kids' menu, an Indian headdress ready to color, comes with crayons, and lists plenty of things to eat, all under $5. Kids can choose from burgers, fried chicken, and Texas-style corn dogs, which are deep-fried cornmeal-covered franks on a stick. Beverages include regular and chocolate milk, hot chocolate, juices, and sodas.

For an appetizer, check out the Frito pie, chips topped with hot chili, cheese, onions, and sour cream, and served right in the bag, just as if you were at a State Fair somewhere in the southwest. The main menu is Tex-Mex, with several types of chicken, fried shrimp, catfish, good burgers, po'boys, quesadillas, and fajitas. Smoked BBQ beef spareribs and chicken fried steaks and chicken, served with creamy gravy and mashed potatoes, round out the offerings. There is a full bar.

EJ'S LUNCHEONETTE

432 6th Avenue (between 9th and 10th Sts.)

(473-5555

A,C,E,B,D,F,Q to West 4th St.

Hours:
Mon-Thu: 8 AM - 11 PM
Fri & Sat: 8 AM - 12 midnight
Sun: 8 AM - 10:30 PM
Breakfast/Brunch: Anytime

AMEX only **$-$$** **Entertainment:** No

We liked the bright shiny atmosphere of EJ's as soon as we walked in. The booths, tin ceilings, 1940s advertisements, and old-fashioned ice cream counter all say family diner, and each of the three locations of this New York favorite is clearly kid-friendly. We are always greeted with a smile, and the cheerful staff never seems to have a problem with pint-sized diners who drop forks, spill milk, and generally make a little more noise than their parents would prefer. What is unexpected is how good the food is. The blue plate specials (served on blue plates) always feature several fish dinners, pastas, soups, and salads.

There is a special kids' menu that includes pancakes, French toast, eggs, burgers, tuna melts, PB&J, grilled cheese, and pasta, plain or with sauce. There are also a lot of dishes on the main menu that appeal to both kids and adults. Several youngsters that we know say this is their favorite restaurant.

As breakfast is served any time, half the menu is devoted to a wide variety of flapjacks, waffles, eggs, and omelets. For drinks, kids can choose from milk, juice, soda, and milk shakes. (Beer, wine, coffee and tea are also available for grown-ups.) And for the clean-plate club, there are rewards of cakes, brownies, pies, and ice cream.

Sam likes the fact that the waiters really do listen to his requests, especially the one for "no green stuff!" He also appreciates the quick service, that it's OK to be a little noisy, and that you don't have to be perfect at dinner, because, after all, EJ's is a diner.

Other locations:
Upper West Side: 477 Amsterdam Ave.
(between 81st & 82nd Sts.) 873-3444
Upper East Side: 1271 3rd Ave.
(at 73rd St.) 472-0600

ELEPHANT & CASTLE

68 Greenwich Ave. (at 7th Ave. & 11th St.)

☎ 243-1400

🚇 1,2,3,9 to 14th St.

Hours:
Breakfast: 8:30 - 11:30 AM
Lunch: 11:30 AM - 5 PM
Dinner:
Sun- Thu: 5 PM- 12 midnight
Fri & Sat: 5 PM - 1 AM

Brunch:
Sat & Sun: 10 AM - 4:30 PM

💳 $-$$ **Entertainment:** No

Elephant & Castle is a cozy eatery where Sam and I go for an easy early dinner. This odd-shaped restaurant is filled with little nooks and crannies and closely-set tables. The wood floors, paneled walls, white tin ceiling, and acoustic guitar music give Elephant & Castle a classic bohemian feel.

The restaurant is named, oddly enough, after a London subway stop named after a London pub named after a Spanish princess, the Infanta de Castile, whose unsuccessful engagement to Charles I of England provoked a war.

Known for its salads, the restaurant also offers burgers, sandwiches, omelets, entrees such as coriander chicken and sliced skirt steak, and pasta dishes. Everything is reasonably priced, with the most expensive entrees and pastas all less than $11. They serve wonderful crèpes for dessert, with your choice of Grand Marnier, strawberry, hot fudge with hazelnuts and whipped cream, and the Casablanca (vanilla ice cream, bananas, and hot fudge).

HUDSON CORNER CAFE

570 Hudson St. (at 11th St.)

☎ 229-2727

🚇 1,9 to Christopher St.;
   A,C,E to 14th St.

Hours:
Mon-Thu: 12 noon - 11 PM
Fri & Sat: 12 noon - 12 midnight
Sun: 12 noon - 10 PM

Brunch: (No reservations)
Sat & Sun: 12 noon - 3 PM

💳 $

Entertainment: Crayons and paper-covered tables

      10+

Dining at the Hudson Corner Cafe is like eating in a large, friendly farmhouse kitchen — oak floors, gingham tablecloths, knickknack cupboards filled with old bottles, and sideboards laden with baskets of vegetables and flowers. Paper and a jar of crayons are on every table. While there isn't a kids' menu, with 15 types of pasta, including old-fashioned spaghetti and meatballs, there's something for everyone. Sam likes to order one of the ten-inch pizzas or a cheeseburger. There is also a range of chicken dishes, pork chops, BBQ ribs, several types of fish, and salads. Milk, juice and soda are available. Sam likes the hot chocolate so much he goes back for seconds and thirds. The accommodating staff will make up a non-menu item such as a grilled cheese. Customers here tend to be a friendly group as likely as not to strike up a conversation with fellow diners. The weekend brunch is quite popular. In warm weather, sit outside in the picket-fenced cafe, complete with flower boxes and a dog leash. Right up the street is the Bleecker Street Playground, which you can visit after you eat.

89

JEKYLL & HYDE

91 7th Ave. S. (between Barrow & Grove Sts.)

📞 989-7701 & 800-992-4933

🚇 1,9 to Christopher St.

Hours:
Lunch/Dinner: 12 noon - 4 AM
Brunch: ($8.95)
Sat & Sun: 11:30 AM - 4 PM

💳 **$$**   **Entertainment:** Yes

Note: Wheelchair accessible but up two steps.

When I suggest to Sam that we go to a Jekyll & Hyde, I am always greeted with a "great!" and a lot of happy jumping up and down. The Eerie Entertainment Company owns seven of these spooky theme restaurants and there are three that we recommend for family dining. All are a fun cross between *Goosebumps* and *Disneyland*, and are truly among the favorite restaurants of all the kids we know.

There are two Jekyll & Hyde restaurants (see the review of the Jekyll & Hyde Club), and both are worth visiting, as they differ. Also owned by this group is the Night Gallery, which puts a different twist on this same "spooky" theme. All three offer a combination of dining and theater-going, and the experience starts when you are greeted at the door. The hosts and the wait staff, through their dress and manner of speaking, personify each restaurant's theme.

The theme of Jekyll & Hyde is an eccentric explorers' club that the fictional Dr. Jekyll founded in 1931 as a meeting place for mad scientists, unorthodox scholars, and other learned types. The walls are decorated with an odd assortment of exotic travel memorabilia mixed with skeletons, masks, and spooky portraits with moving eyes. Television monitors featuring old black and white horror flicks (often without the soundtracks) hang from the ceiling. The sound system favors oldies, TV themes, and rock hits. There is a "laboratory" area, "cannibal safari" cafe, and a library that has hidden doors to the bathroom (a big hit with the kids).

The menu is standard American fare: salads, pasta, chicken, pizza. The food is just OK and expensive for what it is, but that's not really why you come here. We suggest that both kids and adults stick to the basics. Sam likes the eight-inch pizza. The burgers are acceptable, as are the grilled chicken sandwiches and the London fish and chips. Avoid the appetizers and anything priced over $11.95.

While you are eating, actors who roam the restaurant in spooky costumes may stop at your table for a chat. And you never know when a skeleton might start playing the piano, a gargoyle might come alive and talk to you, or the Frankenstein experiment might be reenacted. Don't tell the kids, but there is an audiovisual room with operators who look through hidden cameras while manipulating the mechanical statues. Maybe a skeleton or a sphinx will talk to your child — especially if you've dropped his or her name to the friendly staff.

JOHN'S PIZZERIA

278 Bleecker St. (between 6th & 7th Aves.)

☎ 243-1680

🚇 1,9 to Christopher St.

Hours:

11:30 AM - 12 midnight

Brunch: No

🚭 $ **Entertainment:**

Watching the pizzas being made

Many kids and adults alike rate John's as the best pizza in New York City. Partly it's because the thin-crust pizza is really terrific, but it's also because the friendly helter-skelter activity makes everyone feel right at home. There are 54 varieties of pizza, as well as pastas and salads. Despite the famous "no slices" policy, these pies are so fabulous that customers keep coming back for more. All four locations feature their trademark coal-fired brick ovens, and when kids go over to watch their pizzas being made, the chefs really ham it up. Expect a wait if you go at peak dining times, but even that will be worth it because of the staff's great attitude and the spectacular New York "fold-over"-style pizza (so-called because the best way to manage a slice is to fold it lengthwise). Beverages are beer, wine, and soda. There are no desserts.

The original John's is everything you'd imagine in a Bleecker Street joint. The tables are Formica, the wooden booths are carved with the initials of former patrons, and there's a killer jukebox that

Laverne and Shirley would approve of. While milk is not available at the pizzeria, we had no problem bringing in a carton from the deli a few doors down. John's even supplied the glasses. Note: Half orders of pasta can be ordered for kids.

Other locations: (See reviews.)
Midtown: 260 W. 44th St.
(between Broadway & 8th Ave.)
Note: Telephone number not available as of press time.
Upper East Side: 408 E. 64th St.
(between 1st & York Aves.) 935-2895
Upper West Side: 48 W. 65th St.
(between Central Park W & Columbus Ave.) 721-7001

KATZ'S DELI
205 E. Houston St. (at Ludlow St.)

☎ 254-2246
🚇 F to 2nd Ave.

Hours:
Sun-Tue: 8 AM - 10 PM
Wed-Thu: 8 AM - 11 PM
Fri & Sat: 8 AM - 12 midnight
Dinner specials: 5 - 7:30 PM
Brunch:
Bagels & lox, all day Sat & Sun

$ **Entertainment:** Crayons

On a recent visit to Katz's Deli, Sam's nine-year-old friend Cole said, "Wow! They did a great job decorating this place to look like an old-fashioned deli!" Difficult to comprehend in this era of theme restaurants, Katz's is the real thing, in operation at this location since 1888. A popular location for movie shoots, this is the place where Harry met Sally.

You can opt for table service, which is fast and friendly, or go straight to the deli counter and order à la cafeteria. (If you go to the counter, you'll use the ticket you're handed as you enter the restaurant; each time you order an item of food, the ticket is punched. As you leave, it's tallied at the cashier).

The hot dogs have repeatedly been proclaimed the "Best of New York," and people also rave about the knishes. Our favorites are the giant sandwiches — the dry-cure corned beef is great, and many people claim the pastrami is the best they've ever had. We've never been able to finish one of these monsters, but we know we're not alone — there are stacks of wrapping paper and bags for leftovers. Katz' is the perfect place to try a real New York egg cream. They also have Dr. Brown's sodas and milk (not listed on the menu — just ask).

Yeah, the tables are linoleum and the chairs are a little beat up, but the garlicky pickles are awesome and the great wall of salami is amazing. A sign from decades ago instructs, "Send a salami to your boy in the army." (Say it with a New York accent — it rhymes.) So for an authentic New York deli meal, go to Katz's, and tell the waiter "I'll have some of what she's having!"

PS for kids from Sam: The cashier has a secret stash of lollipops.

LITTLE HANDS PLAYCAFE

433 E. 6th St. (between 1st Ave. & Ave. A)

☎ 388-0957

🚇 N,R to 8th St.;
6 to Astor Place; F to 2nd Ave.

Hours:
Mon-Fri: 10 AM - 8 PM
Sat & Sun: 10 AM - 9 PM

Brunch: No

 $$

Entertainment: Yes

Very East Village with a low-budget decor and a cutting-edge attitude, Little Hands Playcafe is where adults can relax and enjoy a health-conscious menu while their kids play happily and safely. Ideally suited for toddlers to six-year-olds, the street level dining area has a dozen tables, a coffee/sandwich bar, and a front parking area for strollers. The brightly-colored walls are decorated with equally bright wooden happy faces. Adjacent to the tables is a toy-filled corralled area for toddlers and a multilevel Toontown-like playhouse.

The health-food-oriented menu offers kid-sized PB&J or grilled cheese on multigrain bread, pita, or baguette; baby knishes; baby quiches; fruit and granola, priced at $1 – $2.50. Generously-sized combination sandwiches of ham, turkey, brie, tofu spread, and sprouts run $5 to $6. Kids' drinks are served in paper cups with tops to prevent spills, and the European-style coffees are delicious. For dessert, try the cheesecake. Pick up the monthly activity schedule of kids' workshops, which include art, dance, music, yoga, puppet and clown shows, and musical performances.

In addition, there are two scheduled play groups — for six- to 24-month-olds, and for two- to five-year-olds. Most of these activities take place in the downstairs playroom, furnished with beanbag chairs. Fees run from $5 to $8 per event, and registration is suggested.

MAPPAMONDO

<u>Hours</u>:
Sun-Thu: 12 noon - 11 PM
Fri & Sat: 12 noon - 12 midnight
Brunch: See individual locations

   $ **Entertainment:** No

The Mappamondos are a chic little trio of Italian restaurants known for well-prepared, inexpensive pastas ($6.50 to $8). They also offer meat and fish dishes like sautéed chicken breast, veal scaloppine, sliced steak, and grilled tuna, all for $9.50 to $12. A good choice for a simple, no-frills meal out, each of the restaurants has the same basic menu, yet each has its own touch. The staff is young, friendly, and fast; the kitchen has no problem preparing simple or plain versions of dishes for kids. Go before 7:30 PM to avoid lines.

Antipasti include grilled portobello mushrooms, calamari, carpaccio, and some tasty salads, such as mozzarella with tomatoes, roasted red peppers, and basil, and squid marinated in olive oil. Two popular pastas for adults are the Bianchi e Neri, black and white tagliolini in a spicy tomato sauce, and the penne in fresh tomato sauce. We also like the fusilli with tuna, olives and capers, and the spinach and ricotta raviolis (Panzotti Gratinati). To drink, sodas, juices, coffee, beer and wine are offered. Warn the kids to save room for dessert – tiramisu, crème brûlée and profiteroles.

MAPPAMONDO RESTAURANT

11 Abingdon Sq.

(on 8th Ave. between Bank & 12th Sts.)

(675-3100

🚇 1,2,3,9,A,C,E,L to 14th St.

Brunch: No

This, the original location of Mappamondo, is our favorite because it offers a selection of really good pizzas and focaccia. Sixteen tables and 34 diners somehow manage to squeeze into this cute little restaurant, decorated only with a few maps and globes.

MAPPAMONDO DUE

581 Hudson St. (at Bank St.)

(675-7474

🚇 1,2,3,9, A,C,E,L to 14th St.

Brunch: Sat & Sun: 12 noon - 3 PM

This second location of Mappamondo is also a small, simple room, filled to capacity with tables. It doubles in size in the warmer months with the addition of a sidewalk cafe. They don't serve pizza here, but they do have risotto.

MAPPAMONDO TRE

114 MacDougal St.
(between 3rd & Bleecker Sts.)

(674-8900

A,B,C,D,E,F, to West 4th St.

Brunch: Sat & Sun: 12 noon - 3 PM

Mappamondo Tre has only 25 tables, plus a few more on the sidewalk in the warmer months. It, too, is decorated with globes and maps.

MARY ANN'S

80 2nd Ave. (at 5th St.)

(475-5939

6 to Astor Pl.; L to 3rd St.;
N,R to 8th St.

Hours:
Lunch Mon-Fri: 12 noon - 4 PM
Dinner:
Mon-Thu: 4 - 10:30 PM
Fri & Sat: 4 - 11:30 PM
Sun: 4 - 10 PM

Brunch:
Sat & Sun: 12 noon - 4 PM

■ No AMEX $-$$ **Entertainment:** No

Mary Ann's, with four locations in Manhattan, is an ideal choice for good traditional Mexican fare at modest prices. With its "La Bamba" music, handmade tiles and stucco walls, punched tin star-shaped lamps, and Mexican blankets, you almost feel like you're in Tijuana. Be sure to go early — by 8:15 PM, every table will be filled and there will be a crowd at the bar waiting to eat.

First thing, Sam dives into the bottomless bowl of free chips and salsa. The homemade guacamole starter is served in a stone cornmeal grinder. The $3.95 kids' menu provides large servings of tacos, enchiladas, cheese quesadillas, chicken fajitas, or crispy flauta chicken rolls, all with rice, beans, or French fries. All the other dishes are ample, too — we never leave hungry.

The sizzling fajitas, available in steak, chicken or vegetarian variations, served with a lot of fanfare, are probably the most popular dish on the menu, but you really can't go wrong with any of the classic Mexican combination plates. We have especially enjoyed the Santa Fe sirloin burritos, the taco and enchilada specials, and the Mary Ann's combo, a shrimp burrito and chicken tostado. Vegetarian varieties are also available. For something a little different, try the camarones Veracruz, a delicious preparation of sautéed jumbo shrimp. Like most of the other dishes, these are served with generous sides of rice, beans, and salad.

Other locations:
Chelsea: 116 8th Ave.
(at 16th St.) 633-0877
Upper East Side: 1503 2nd Ave.
(at 78th St.) 249-6165 (See review.)
Upper West Side: 2452 Broadway
(at 91st St.) 877-0132

MIRACLE GRILL

112 First Ave. (between 6th & 7th Sts.)

☎ 254-2353

🚇 6 to Astor Pl.; N,R to 8th St.; F to 2nd Ave.

MIRACLE BAR & GRILL

415 Bleecker St. (between Bank & 11th Sts.)

☎ 924-1900

🚇 1,9 to Christopher St.; A,C,E,2,3 to 14th St.

Hours:
Dinner:
Mon-Thu: 5:30 - 11:30 PM
Fri & Sat: 5:30 PM - 12 midnight
Sun: 5:30 - 11 PM
Brunch:
Sat & Sun: 11:30 AM - 3 PM

 \$\$ **Entertainment:** No

   6+

For many years, Miracle Grill has been known for innovative southwestern cuisine. Once home to celebrity chef Bobby Flay, who went on to open Mesa Grill, the kitchen continues to serve food bursting with flavor and spice. The laid-back East Village location, with its plain "casa" interior of exposed brick and sponge-painted light brown walls, natural wood flooring, and scuffed-up black western-decorated tables, has long been a good place for kids. The back garden is particularly nice in the summer.

At the site of the former Cottonwood Cafe, the new West Village Miracle Grill has a spare, slightly

100

sophisticated Santa Fe decor, with paper-covered tables and a twinkling of light jazz in the background. Larger, it has two dining rooms, a bigger kitchen, and a more extensive menu.

Items that kids might want to order are the grilled chicken breast, the chicken fajitas, and the black Angus steak. These can be prepared plain with the special sauces on the side. The tender grilled pork chops, for instance, come with a sweet mole-like orange-ancho recado sauce, which some kids may not appreciate. The kitchen will substitute fries or mashed potatoes as side dishes.

Additional items that we have enjoyed at the West Village location include the southwestern spring roll, a yummy peanut-flavored coleslaw wrapped in a soft tortilla, the wonderful barbecued salmon with ancho glaze and spinach, and the southwestern saffron risotto topped with wood-grilled shrimp. Kids will like the sirloin burgers and you can order half portions of baked macaroni and cheese; Sam prefers the enchilada sauce on the side for this one.

Both locations serve the Miracle quesadilla filled with zucchini, corn, cheese, and guacamole. Unfortunately, at the East Village location these cannot be ordered with only cheese. The West Village site, however, usually is able to make special orders for kids with cheese or chicken, in both half and whole sizes. Other quesadillas available on the West Village menu are goat cheese, roast duck, and a tantalizing wild mushroom served with a fresh fruit chutney.

MOUSTACHE WEST VILLAGE
90 Bedford St. (between Barrow & Grove Sts.)
☎ 229-2220
🚇 1,9 to Christopher St.

MOUSTACHE EAST VILLAGE
265 E. 10th St. (between 1st Ave. & Ave. A)
☎ 228-2022
🚇 L to 1st Ave., 6 to Astor Pl.

Hours:
12 noon - 12 midnight
Brunch: No

 $ **Entertainment:** No

To many, dining in Greenwich Village means discovering wonderfully good, ethnic food in a bohemian setting. Those who find their way to Moustache will not be disappointed. Tucked away on narrow Bedford Street, this tiny restaurant, with its 12 copper tables, is a gem. The decor is simple, with an Arabic tapestry against a brick wall; the views of the food being prepared, the unusual aromas, and the Turkish background music set the atmosphere. Lively and casual, both the staff and the clientele seem happy and friendly. We must caution you though — the best time to eat here is from 4:30 to 6:30 PM. All the tables fill up by 7, and the staff gets quite busy.

Moustache is known for its "pitza," which are crisp pizzas, with a crust of pita bread, served on a wooden paddle. Perfectly meal-sized for a child, they are also nice as a shared appetizer. Oven-fresh pita bread comes to the table puffed up like a pillow. Dip it into hummos (ground chick peas with tahini), babaganough (eggplant mash), or yogurt sauce. The fresh spinach and cheese pie is popular as is ouzi, a chicken pilaf/vegetable stew in a phyllo pie with almonds, sweet raisins, and spices. We especially recommend the grilled baby lamb ribs. Tender and full of wood smoke flavor, they are served with a minty tomato and cucumber salad. For dessert, don't miss the basboussa, a rich, dense semolina cake, the four-inch-long flaky phyllo roll filled with raisins, chopped walnuts, and honey, or the terrific pistachio ice cream.

NIGHT GALLERY CAFE
117 7th Ave. S.
(between Christopher & 10th Sts.)

(675-0350 & 800-421-6483

🚇 1,9 to Christopher St.

Hours:
Lunch & Dinner: 11:30 AM - 2 AM
Brunch:
Sat & Sun: 11:30 AM - 4 PM

 \$\$ **Entertainment:** Yes

The hosts of the Night Gallery Cafe, the newest restaurant opened by the Eerie Entertainment Company, will make you and your kids feel quite welcome. An art gallery of the "macabre," the walls are lined with sculptures and sci-fi paintings. A large bar in the front appears to be right out of *Star Wars*. To the side is a nine-screen wall of video monitors featuring non-stop computer photo animation and multimedia effects. And scattered throughout the restaurant are larger-than-life statues that come to life and talk to you at any given moment.

The menu is a step up from the fare at the Jekyll & Hyde restaurants. Besides the burgers, pizza, pastas, and chicken dishes, there are entrees such as grilled yellowfin tuna, pumpkin tortellini, filet mignon, and lobster. The tradition of 250 different types of beer continues here, but watch out... some are pricey. In addition, there are a few concocted drinks, some without alcohol. The dessert menu has a haunting selection of death-to-the-diet possibilities.

The highlight of the evening for Sam and his friends is the impromptu gallery tour, which the theatrically-clad hosts will arrange if the restaurant is not too full (early evening is a good time). And, they tell us, the artwork is really for sale.

PATSY'S PIZZERIA

67 University Pl. (between 10th & 11th Sts.)

☎ 533-3500

🚇 L,N,R,4,5,6 to Union Sq.

Hours:
Sun-Thu: 12 noon - 11 PM
Fri & Sat: 12 noon - 12 midnight
Brunch: No

 $-$$ **Entertainment:** No

In the first quarter of this century, several young Italian pizza chefs, including John of John's Pizzeria, Tottono of Coney Island, and Patsy Lancieri, learned their craft at Gennaro Lombardi's restaurant. These chefs then went on to open their own, now famous, pizzerias. The one Patsy Lancieri opened in 1933 in East Harlem is still in business, serving not only pizza but also salads, soups, pastas, and desserts. His nephew, Patsy Grimaldi, subsequently went on to open Patsy Grimaldi's. Recently, four branches of Patsy's Pizzeria have opened in Manhattan, all of which we recommend for families.

Patsy's Pizzeria offers brick-oven pizzas and an extensive menu that includes appetizers, salads, and pasta. The pizza ovens are in the dining rooms, where you can watch the chefs at work. Pizzas cost $10.95 and $12.95 and toppings are an additional $2 each. The small pizza is certainly big enough for two kids. Salads and pastas are available in individual and family-sized portions. Roughly twice the price of the generous single

105

servings, the "big bowl" family orders are an excellent buy, easily serving a family of four.

We love going to the University Place location of Patsy's with its trattoria-in-the-Old-Country feel. Large windows with small ornate balconies overlook University Place, and the floor is made of a pretty tile mosaic. As at the other locations, they make flavorful pizza with a light crust. Individual or economically priced family-sized portions of salads, the daily pasta, and soup specials are also available.

Other locations: (See reviews.)
Murray Hill: 509 3rd Ave.
(at 34th St.) 689-7500
Upper East Side: 1312 2nd Ave.
(at 69th St.) 639-1000
Upper West Side: 64 W. 74th St.
(at Columbus Ave.) 579-3000

SASSY'S SLIDERS

163 1st Ave. (at E. 10th St.)

☎ 228-2900

🚇 L to 1st Ave.; 6 to Astor Pl.

Hours:
Sun-Thurs: 11 AM - 11 PM
Fri/Sat: 11 AM - 1 AM
Brunch: No

 $　　**Entertainment:** No

Note: No restrooms

On the wall at Sassy's Sliders is a sign defining a Slider: "A perfectly proportioned bite-size burger that once tasted is irresistible. Usually eaten in multiples." While the food here is served likety-split, none of the other fast food stereotypes apply. Much thought has gone into each detail, from the organic ingredients in each of these yummy little 79¢ patties to the retro decor and the light background jazz. And the sign is right: the specialty of the house, made with beef, turkey or vegetables and served with browned onions, pickles and ketchup on a mini bun, is so good that I found it impossible to eat just one. Sam also loves the hand-cut fries ($1.19) and recommends the frozen custard shakes, which are made from a special egg-enriched ice cream.

You sit at turquoise and stainless steel counters on stools that spin and are just the right height for kids. Decorating the shiny white walls are photos of burger joints all across America that formed the inspiration for young Sassy's dad to open his own "griddled burger" place. (Their names alone, including *Bimbo's*, the *Bun Boy*, and the *Cozy Inn*, are a charming roll call of Americana). And if you stop by on a weekend, you may just meet 11-year-old Sassy herself helping out.

SECOND AVENUE KOSHER DELI

156 2nd Ave. (at 10th St.)

(677-0606

🚇 6 to Astor Pl. ; N,R to 8th St.

Hours:
Sun-Thu: 7 AM - 12 midnight
Fri & Sat: 7 AM - 2 AM
Brunch: No

💳 AMEX only **$** **Entertainment:** No

There was a time when this area was called the Lower East Side (instead of the East Village). It was a place where many Jewish immigrants made their first homes in America. The Second Avenue Deli captures the spirit of that time with a friendliness that treats every diner as family and with food so good it tastes like "Mama must have made it!" Old Worldly in atmosphere, despite renovations that were almost complete as of press time, the deli features tables trimmed with dark wood, a copper-colored ceiling above simply framed mirrors, and a brand-new tiled floor — all of such classic "deli" design that they seem to have always been there. These are all as the late owner, Abe Lebewohl, would have wanted, as he had planned this renovation down to the new light fixtures.

The kosher food served here is also part of preserving a tradition. As you scan the enormous menu, large bowls of great dill pickles and sweet coleslaw appear on your table. We are still discovering new items on the menu, but it's hard not to go back to the heavenly corned beef — so tender that even a child with new braces won't have a problem. The twin double is a good item to order for two kids: two tall sandwiches, one corned beef and the other pastrami, on junior sized rolls. The open sandwich medley ($29.90) lets you try everything and will feed a table full of hungry kids. It consists of corned beef, tongue, roast beef, turkey, pastrami, the deli's famous chopped liver, eggs, salami, and potato salad. "You gotta try" their famous chicken soup with a matzoth ball the size of a baseball. The potato knish is even bigger. Irresistible potato pancakes come with fresh homemade applesauce. Still hungry? There's lots more, but for kids who are not adventurous the freshly ground beef burgers are great, and there are terrific hot dogs and lots of chicken dishes. The Second Avenue Deli is kosher, so butter and milk are not served. Service is fast but never rushed, and the staff is quick to echo Mama — "Did you have enough to eat?"

SILVER SPURS

771 Broadway (at E. 9th St.)

☏ 473-5517/8

🚇 N,R to 8th St.; 6 to Astor Pl.

Hours:
Breakfast: 7 - 11 AM
Lunch/Dinner: 11 AM - 11 PM
Brunch: No

💳 $ **Entertainment:** No

Not a bit like the Silver Spurs Saloon of Bonnie & Clyde fame, this is really just a little sandwich shop with small butcher block tables and a counter with stools. There are lots of basic, economically-priced options on the menu — salads, omelets, and sandwiches, including chicken cutlets, tuna salad, and PB&J. We tend to order their consistently-good burgers, ($3.95 for the basic beef, turkey or veggie), which can be prepared almost any way you like them.

Other location: 490 La Guardia Pl.
(at Houston St.) 228-2333. (See review.)

THREE OF CUPS

83 1st Ave. (at 5th St.)

(388-0059

F to 2nd Ave; 6 to Bleecker St.

Hours:
Sun-Thu: 6 PM - 1 AM
Fri & Sat: 6 PM - 2 AM

Brunch:
Sat & Sun: 12 noon - 4 PM

 $-$$ Entertainment: No

Note: Wheelchair accesible but up one step.

Sam thinks that Three of Cups, with its medieval decor, is a cool place for pizza. We usually sit at one of the window tables, where we can watch the East Village street action, the activity in the restaurant, and the pizzas being made in the large stone oven. Families with young children favor the back dining room because kids can roam about there and it's a little more private.

The medieval theme is evident in the leaded-glass walls and tall ladderback stools in the small bar; the wall lamps are shaped like torches and lances, and the old-fashioned chandelier is shaped like a crown. Tall red hurricane candles flicker on the dark wood tables, which are surrounded by car chairs.

The aroma of baking pizzas will put a sp
you from the moment you walk in. There
different varieties from basic to eclectic, s
the shrimp with pesto white pie, and the

salad with vinaigrette served on a warm crust and topped with mozzarella. The restaurant is well known for the Mickey, a charred baked potato loaded with butter, definitely worth trying. The reasonably priced menu includes antipasti, several nice salads, many pastas (the kitchen will prepare half orders of plain pastas for kids), and entrees such as chicken, steak, salmon, and pork chops. There are sodas, milk (ask), wine, and a full bar; the service is fast and friendly.

TIME CAFE WEST

87 7th Ave. S. (at Barrow St.)

(220-9100

1,9 to Houston St.

Hours:
Self-serve breakfast:
Mon-Fri: 8 - 11:30 AM
Lunch: Mon-Fri: 12 noon - 5:30 PM
Dinner:
Sun-Wed: 5:30 PM - 2 AM
Thu-Sat: 5:30 PM - 4 AM

Brunch:
Sat & Sun: 10:30 AM - 5:30 PM

 $$

Entertainment:
Crayons, coloring books; (you may
have to ask for them), postcards,
kids magazines.

Note: Roof garden open during warmer months.

Time Cafe has opened a second location in the
West Village. Decorated with a "Go West" theme,
it features a wall-sized photo mural of the Mojave
Desert and cactus planters in the place of flowers
on the tables. Reservations are highly recom-
mended as this popular new spot is about a quar-
ter the size of the NoHo original. The restaurant
has an engaging upscale but casual atmosphere,
welcomes children, provides excellent service
and offers diversions such as kids' magazines,
crayons, and coloring books.

As of press time, the menu is the same as
the original Time Cafe's, with pizzas, barbecued
free-range chicken, and salmon with sesame
crust. For lunch, Sam likes to order a hot choco-
late and one of the big burgers; adults may enjoy

a fruit smoothie and a salad. The arugula salad with beets, walnuts, and gorgonzola and the cucumber yogurt salad with feta cheese are both delicious. Other appetizers that make great light meals are the tuna rolls with avocado, or the grilled steak, shrimp, and chicken tapas. For more information, see the review of Time Cafe.

TSUNAMI

70 W. 3rd St.
(between LaGuardia Pl. & Thompson St.)

☎ 475-7770

🚇 A,B,C,D,E,F,Q to West 4th St./
Washington Sq.; N,R to 8th St.

Hours:
Lunch: 12 noon - 4 PM
Dinner: 4 PM - 12 midnight
Brunch: No

💳 $$-$$$ Entertainment: No

Upon entering Tsunami, you leave the bustle of New York for the serenity of Japan. The restaurant is simply decorated with spot-lit birch trees and handmade paper sconces. Studied dried flower arrangements are framed on the back wall. A blue paneled ceiling sculpture is an abstract interpretation of the restaurant's name: Tsunami, loosely translated, means giant wave.

Dominating the center of the restaurant is New York's only water canal sushi bar. About 15 feet in length, the canal encircles the large oval bar, and the chefs prepare the food in the center. Diners sit all around at the laquered copper counter. Wooden boats bearing freshly-made sushi float by, and if you see something you wish to try, you simply lift the plate off the boat. The color of the plate determines its cost (there's a chart to guide you) and the plates are tallied by your waiter. On Monday through Wednesday nights, Tsunami offers an all-you-can-eat sushi special for $23.50.

115

KIDS EAT NEW YORK

In addition to sushi and sashimi, there are several traditional Japanese dishes that your children might enjoy — the steak teriyaki, grilled chicken, broiled yellowtail tuna, shrimp and vegetable tempura fried in a light batter. Soba noodles are available warm or chilled as part of a delicious multicolored salad. The hearty Tsunami ramen is a generous bowl of shellfish and noodles in broth. Desserts include chocolate cake, ginger cheesecake, brandy flambe tempura Alaska, and ice cream (ginger, red bean and green tea).

The restaurant is very clean and the dress is upscale casual. A small jazz group performs on Friday and Saturday nights, beginning around 8 PM. Even if you're not eating sushi, it's fun to sit at the counter; menu items are served there as well. Service is attentive and very friendly to kids. We know one child who likes this restaurant so much, he had his birthday party here. (When we asked how the chefs get into the sushi bar, our waitress answered, quite seriously: "Jump — they practice at night after everyone goes home!")

TWO BOOTS

Named for the twin boots of Italy and Louisiana, Two Boots has grown to a restaurant and three take out pizzerias all in Greenwich Village. The menu at the restaurant also features a combination of Italian and Cajun cuisine, and is designed with kids in mind. All four locations serve up a wide, eccentric variety of pizza in four sizes with toppings that include vegetables (broccoli, eggplant, spinach, roasted peppers, sun-dried tomatoes) and seafood (calamari, crawfish, and BBQ shrimp), as well as the standard cheese, pepperoni, etc.

TWO BOOTS RESTAURANT

37 Avenue A (between 2nd & 3rd Sts.)

☎ 505-2276

🚇 F to 2nd Ave.

Hours:
Sun-Thu: 12 noon - 12 midnight
Fri & Sat: 12 noon - 1 AM

Brunch:
Sat & Sun: 12 noon - 4 PM

💳 $

Entertainment: Crayons, coloring books, sketch pads

The menus here all have different covers — and they're all drawings done by young patrons of the restaurant. The walls, too, are an ever-changing display of works created during meal time at Two Boots. The owners, who have school kids of their own, provide coloring books, sketch pads, and crayons, as well as pencils, if homework is on the evening's agenda. Service is attentive,

117

and the staff honestly loves children. The kids' menu ($3.95) features mini ravioli, spaghetti, chicken fingers, fish sticks and Pizza Face, a small pie decorated with an edible face. Somewhere around 5:00 or 5:30, the regular lunch offerings give way to the dinner fare, which includes soups, salads, appetizers (such as Creole popcorn and mussels in wine sauce), and Cajun po'boys (catfish, chicken, and vegetarian). There are daily specials and entrees such as blackened chicken, butternut squash ravioli, and pasta jambalaya (made with chicken, shrimp, and andouille). We recommend the catfish, either pecan-crusted or sautéed with capers, and don't forget to try the jalapeno cornbread. The kids' sodas are served in boot-shaped mugs. If you are looking for a swank night out, this is not the place for you. Two Boots is true funky East Village style, decorated with ropes of garlic, strings of tacky plastic pizza lights, and lots of boots.

TWO BOOTS PIZZERIAS

These three take-out locations of Two Boots have only limited seating. Although hours and many other details are the same for all three, each one has its own personality.

Hours: 11:30 AM - 12:30 AM
Brunch: No

 AMEX only **$** **Entertainment:** No

TWO BOOTS PIZZERIA
44 Avenue A (between 3rd & 4th Sts.)

(254-1919

F to 2nd Ave.

Note: No booster seats and no rest rooms.

Across the street from the Two Boots restaurant is the new, larger location of Two Boots Pizzeria, featuring bright red booths (four large, and two enormous), bright green wainscoting, a ceiling trimmed bright yellow, George Jetson lamps, ropes of garlic, and vintage rock music. There are two more stand-up tables and a neighborhood notice column. In addition to the core pizza menu are specials such as the kid-sized "Pizza Face", the "Poseidon Adventure" (shrimp, crawfish, and calamari pizza) plus calzones and salad.

Downstairs is the new "Den of Cin" party room. Reminiscent of a suburban basement rec room, it has an eight-foot video screen, surround-sound stereo, and a 1960s decor complete with beanbag chairs and couches. It's available for private party rentals (777-BOOT).

Adjoining the pizzeria is the new Two Boots Video (254-1441), a unique operation where you can order both a pizza and a movie for delivery. With a collection that includes lots of kids' flicks at maybe the lowest prices in the neighborhood ($3/features, $2/nonfeatures) and great hours (open 'til 1 AM most nights), it is already a big hit. Check out the daily specials such as the 4x3=10 (Fridays: rent four movies for three days for ten bucks).

TWO BOOTS TO GO GO
74 Bleecker St.
(between Broadway & Lafayette St.)

(777-1033

🚇 6 to Bleecker St.

Note: No booster seats and no rest rooms.

Offering the basic Two Boots pizza and calzone menu, this location has two small counters with stools and one large booth that can squeeze in six. What with the bustling NYU street action, this is a fun place to get a slice. The decor is 1950s trailer park kitsch and despite the crowds, the help always seems friendly and happy.

TWO BOOTS TO GO WEST
75 Greenwich Ave. (at 7th Ave.)

(633-9096

🚇 1,9 to Christopher St.

Note: Booster seats are available. There are no rest rooms.

Shaped like a slice of pizza, Two Boots To Go West serves up all the famous Two Boots pizza styles, as well as po'boys and sloppy joes. Not to be confused with a real restaurant, this is an OK stop for a quick bite. There are five small tables and stand-up counters along the side, but the best seats are at the counter in the "point" of the room, which has a great view of the 7th Avenue doings.

YE WAVERLY INN

16 Bank St. (at Waverly Pl.)

☏ 929-4377

🚇 1,2,3 to 14th St.

Hours:

Lunch:
Mon-Fri: 11:30 AM - 3:30 PM
Dinner:
Mon-Thu: 5 - 10:30 PM
Fri & Sat: 5 - 11:30 PM
Sun: 5 - 10 PM

Brunch ($11.50):
Sat & Sun: 11 AM - 3:30 PM

💳 $$

Entertainment:
No (except for hauntings)

Note: No kids menu but will do special orders.
For wheelchair access call in advance to open side
entrance.

When kids reach a certain age, somewhere around
six or seven, they develop a real interest in any-
thing spooky, hence the success of *Goosebumps*,
and *Are You Afraid of the Dark*. Well, there is a
restaurant in the West Village that may really be
haunted, Ye Waverly Inn. We had to check this out,
of course, and I admit we were a little skeptical —
until we stepped into Room No. 16. We all felt it,
but Sam described it best when he said he felt
"heavy." There was a sort of presence, but it
seemed friendly and we had no problem spending a
lovely evening, sharing a delicious meal.

Built in 1844, the building was used as a carriage
house, inn, and tavern until 1920, when it was
established as a restaurant. Owing to a fire in
1996 (which, oddly enough, spared the ghost's
quarters), the Inn closed for a few months for

renovation. It has, however, retained its colonial-era feel, with low ceilings, floral wallpaper, and charming antiques. The working fireplaces are a delight to sit near in the winter, and the pretty garden a pleasure in the summer. As the tables are set fairly close together, this restaurant is not suitable for rambunctious younger children. Sam and his friend brought a pack of cards and an assortment of toy spiders to entertain themselves, and this was no problem.

While there is no children's menu per se, the hearty American fare provides many suitable choices. The inn is known for its traditional favorites — chicken pot pie; roasted turkey with cornbread stuffing, cranberry sauce, and gravy; southern fried chicken; and French meatloaf in a flaky crust. Tender filet mignon, savory grilled chicken, and baby back ribs are other options. All are served with a choice of salad or vegetable, including great mashed potatoes. The kitchen not only splits orders between kids but will substitute pasta for the vegetable, as well as prepare items "plain." Portions are so generous that two adults would be satisfied sharing a main course, provided they each begin with an appetizer. The wild mushrooms with polenta and the warm asparagus salad with potatoes and pine nuts are starter standouts. During the week, the early-bird special at $13.50 is an excellent buy. And do go early; the tables usually fill up by 7:30 PM.

CHELSEA, GRAMERCY PARK & MURRAY HILL

The large area known as **Chelsea** extends from 14th to 34th Streets and from the Hudson River to Third Avenue.

The **Flatiron** district is named after the historic triangular building located at the point where Broadway crosses Fifth Avenue at 23rd Street; it extends from Sixth Avenue to Park Avenue and from 14th Street to 23rd Street.

The little section called **Gramercy Park** is bordered by 23rd and 17th Streets and runs from Park Avenue to Third Avenue.

Above that is **Murray Hill**, which includes the blocks from 3rd Avenue to 6th Avenue and from 23rd Street to 34th Street.

RESTAURANTS

ATTRACTIONS with RESTAURANTS

AMERICA

9 E. 18th St. (between 5th Ave. & Union Sq. W.)

(505-2110

🚆 L,N,R,4,5,6, to 14 St./Union Sq.

Hours:
Lunch/Dinner:
Sun-Thu: 11:30 AM - 11:30 PM
Fri & Sat: 11:30 AM - 12:30 PM
Brunch:
Sat & Sun: 11:30 AM - 4 PM

💳 $$ **Entertainment:** Coloring books
and crayons; Kids storytelling:
Sat. 12:30 - 2:30 PM.
Magic shows/ballonmaking:
Sun. 12 - 4 PM.

Note: Wheelchair accessible door on side. Notify restaurant personnel for assistance and to disable the alarm.

America the restaurant, which specializes in food from all over the country, opened in 1985, and it has been steadily attracting diners of all ages ever since. The decor of the cavernous space celebrates all things American. George (Washington) and Abe (Lincoln) preside over a table in one corner of the large platform bar area in the rear, and the Statue of Liberty holds up her torch in the other. Oversized pastel paintings of an American eagle and the New York harbor cover the side walls. Neon jet streams trail across the 25-foot-high ceiling and spot-lit stars shine on the floor.

The equally enormous menu starts with breakfast (eggs, omelets, pancakes), which is available all day, and lists each dish with its city or state of origin. Did you know that meatloaf is from

Missouri, turkey burgers from North Carolina, fried catfish from Mississippi, and fluffernutters from Las Vegas? (Las Vegas?)

Appetizers range from California sushi rolls (Venice) and oysters Rockefeller (New Orleans) to hush puppies (Savannah) and potato skins (Sun Valley). The popular Frito Pie is a mix of tortilla chips, cheese and chili served in a pie-shaped dish. There is no kids' menu but the kitchen will do half orders and smaller portions. The several different types of pasta include macaroni and cheese; there is also a staggering number of salads. In addition to the daily specials, one can choose from pizza, burgers, lamb or pork chops, chicken prepared several ways, half racks of ribs, New York or T-bone steaks or an entire traditional turkey dinner. Among the seafood dishes are tuna, salmon, jambalaya shrimp (Texas), and fish and chips (Austin ???). Sandwiches include Dodger (hot) dogs (LA) and PB&J (Peoria). Many dessert selections round out the menu.

America's staff goes out of its way to welcome kids and their families. On the floor, next to the maitre d' stand, is a large basket filled with coloring books and crayons. (Don't be shy about asking for them — sometimes the staff forgets to offer.) Weekend afternoons find lots of special kid-type events like storytelling, balloon-making, and magic shows. Service is fast and considerate, and everything is very clean. So if you want to know where the cheeseburger is from, and also have a tasty experience, we highly recommend America.

BENDIX DINER

219-221 8th Ave. (at 21st St.)

☎ 366-0560

🚇 C,E to 23rd; 1,9 to 23rd St.

Hours:
8 AM - 11 PM

Brunch: No

▬ **$-$$**   **Entertainment:** No

When asked why the Bendix Diner is his favorite restaurant, our ten-year-old friend Leigh put it succinctly: "Because they have everything I want to eat." Long a popular food spot for that very reason, its recent expansion means that there is no longer always a wait for a table. We love the colorful cartoony illustrations of New York on the walls and the funny "Get Fat" logo. Kids quickly feel at home in the bustling coffee shop atmosphere. Good, cheap food (although sometimes a little greasy) is served up with fast service (sometimes a little chaotic). The menu is American diner with a dash of Thai. This unusual combination allows the kids to have burgers, fries, and a shake, while adults munch on pad Thai, Yaki soba (stir fried soba noodles with chicken and vegetables), or gai tom ka — coconut milk soup flavored with lemongrass. Kids usually like the Thai-style chicken satay (chicken barbecued on a wooden skewer) or the wontons (steamed or fried), as well as sandwich standbys such as grilled cheese, turkey, steak, chicken and tuna melts. Breakfast, available anytime, includes bagels and lox, eggs, granola, and stacks of fruit-filled buckwheat pancakes that are quite a challenge to finish. No liquor is served, but BYO is welcomed. Note: Candy treats for well-behaved kids.

E. Village location: 167 1st Ave.
(between 10th & 11th Sts.) 260-4220

CHAT 'N CHEW

10 E. 16th St.
(between 5th Ave. & Union Square W.)
☎ 243-1616
🚇 L,N,R,4,5,6 to 14th St./Union Sq.

Hours:
Lunch:
Mon-Fri: 11:30 AM - 3:30 PM
Dinner: 5:30 - 10 PM

Brunch:
Sat & Sun: 10 AM - 4 PM

 AMEX only **$** **Entertainment:** No

      6+

Chat 'n Chew is best described as a feed store for people. The rustic decor is 1950s country store complete with old-fashioned advertising signs, class photos, wagon wheels, and shutters. The food here is basic and served in large portions on linoleum tables that can bear up to any child's spills, and the staff is more than tolerant of rambunctious kids. The kids' menu features favorites such as honey-fried chicken, burgers, and grilled cheese, all with fries. The regular menu has additional dishes that appeal to children — pork chops, macaroni and cheese, meatloaf, and roast turkey. Don't miss the blackboard of daily specials that range from mahimahi to banana fritters. Sam loves the thick milk shakes, the attentive service, and the large candy bowl by the door.

129

CHELSEA GRILL

135 8th Ave. (between 16th & 17th Sts.)

☎ 242-5336

🚇 A,C,E,L to 14th St.;
1,9, to 18th St.

Hours:
11:30 AM - 11 PM Daily
$9.95 Prix Fixe:
Sun-Thu: 5 - 8:30 PM
Fri & Sat: 5 - 7:30 PM

Brunch:
Sat & Sun: 11:30 AM - 4 PM

▬ $ **Entertainment:** No

The Chelsea Grill recently underwent a transformation, changing from a bar-eatery to a family-friendly restaurant. That and its excellent value are packing the diners in. But don't worry — if you go early (before 7:30 PM), you'll have no problem getting a table.

The decor is clean and simple — a bar in front and a roomy dining area in the back with wood floors, exposed brick walls, ceiling fans, and tables and booths. As of this writing, the garden was being redesigned for outdoor dining. Service is fast and the management has made it a point to welcome kids.

A separate children's menu would be redundant here as the regular fare has been designed with grown-up kids in mind. For $6 you can choose a ten-ounce beefsteak burger, a turkey burger, a fresh vegetable burger, or chicken breast on a bun, with fries. For 50 cents a topping, you can add cheese, chili, bacon, salsa, guacamole, marinara or

BBQ sauce. Smaller (regular-sized) burgers are $4.75 and a foot-long hot dog with waffle fries is $4.25. Other choices include bar-type appetizers (nachos, buffalo wings, guacamole with chips), Caesar or house salads, and blackboard specials. On Wednesday, Pizza and Pasta Night, the specials include linguine or cheese ravioli in a tomato sauce, fettuccine Alfredo, and penne in vodka sauce. On weekends, brunch specials for under $6 include pancakes, French toast, three-egg omelets, and steak and eggs. In addition, the kitchen promises to make every effort to customize any dish to your requirements. Beverages include milk and the biggest sodas we have ever seen — 32 oz. for $2.00 with free refills. There are daily activities at the bar — Monday, for instance, is *Star Trek* Night.

We recommend the Chelsea Grill for a casual family meal. The food, while basic, is good, and the check won't break the bank.

DUKE'S

99 E. 19th St. (at Park Ave. S.)

☏ 260-2922

🚇 6 to 23rd St.;
L,N,R,4 to 14th St./Union Sq.

Hours:
Mon-Fri: 12 noon - 11 PM
Sat & Sun: 3 PM - 12 midnight
Brunch (not in summer):
Sat & Sun: 11 AM - 4 PM

Entertainment: No

 6+

Walking into Duke's is like walking into a local BBQ place on Route 66 somewhere west of the Mississippi. It looks and feels like it has been there for generations, but in fact this restaurant has been open only since 1994. It's actually too vintage-looking for my taste, but Sam and his friends disagree. They love the old rock and roll singles that decorate the front bar and the 978 bottle caps (Yes, Sam counted them!) nailed to the kitchen window ledge. And while I wouldn't bring the grandparents here, Sam has a good time because the staff is quite friendly to kids and lets them run around as much as they wish. Duke's may also be popular for its good kids' menu with chicken fingers, macaroni and cheese, burgers, BBQ, and fried fish, all with fries or mashed potatoes. And, from 5 to 7 PM, kids seven years old and under eat for free.

The main menu features BBQ chicken, fish, beef and ribs — all cooked with mesquite, apple, and hickory hardwoods. There are also salads, sandwiches, and sides such as corn on the cob and delicious coleslaw. The prices are very reasonable and the food is OK. Besides the full bar, there are milk, juice, sodas, and root beer floats, all served in mugs. Desserts include ice cream and chocolate pecan or banana cream pie.

EIGHTEENTH & EIGHTH

159 8th Ave. (at 18th St.)

☎ 242-5000

🚇 A,C,E,L to 14th St.;
   1,9 to 18th St.

Hours:
Breakfast: 9 AM - 4 PM
Lunch:
Mon-Fri: 9 AM - 5 PM
Sat & Sun: 2 PM - 12 midnight
Dinner: 5 PM - 12 midnight
Brunch: Sat & Sun: 9 AM - 4 PM

$-$$ ▭ No AMEX   **Entertainment:** No

Eighteenth & Eighth is a cozy little gem of a cafe in the heart of predominantly gay west Chelsea's restaurant row. From the street you'd never guess what a clean, pretty place this is, but it's a well-known neighborhood secret and so the little tables with white paper-covered tablecloths fill up as early as 5 PM. Meals here are enhanced by the thoughtful design touches — the color of the blond wood cafe chairs, for example, is echoed in the tile floor. Cream-colored walls are accented with a collection of colorful photographs and sur-realistic landscapes. Pretty dried flower arrange-ments stand on either side of the doorway, and high up on one wall is a collection of ceramic teapots and cookie jars.

KIDS EAT NEW YORK

The food here emphasizies fresh, organic ingredients (even the ice cubes are made from purified water), and there are plenty of kid choices on the menu. The $5.50 oversized burger with fries is a popular selection. The many sandwiches include grilled chicken, roast beef, and peanut butter, and the kitchen will make grilled cheese and half portions of plain pasta on request. The specials feature such comfort food as pork chops, steak, and meatloaf. For grownups, there are a variety of salads and soups, quite a few vegetarian dishes, and a number of seafood entrees. Everything is well prepared and reasonably priced. Drinks include freshly-squeezed OJ, apple juice, pink lemonade, sodas, shakes and milk (including soy milk). There is a full bar, as well as delicious coffees and teas. For dessert, treat the kids to some gelato or a choice of pies, carrot cake, or chocolate torte.

Although Eighteenth & Eighth doesn't take reservations, they will try to accommodate you if you call ahead. Otherwise plan on a wait, especially around 6:30-7 PM or at brunch time on weekends. The service is very friendly and children are welcomed, but the tables are close together, so we don't recommend it for little kids.

EMPIRE DINER

210 10th Ave. (at 22nd St.)

(243-2736
A,C,E to 23rd St.

<u>Hours:</u>
Open 24 hours a day
Breakfast Special ($3.95):
Mon-Fri: 6 - 10 AM
Brunch: Sun 12 noon - 4 PM

$$ **Entertainment:** Piano music

Note: Wheelchair access up a few steps; restaurant personnel will assist. During the summer there is sidewalk dining, which is completely accessible.

Originally built in the 1920s for its current site, the Empire Diner epitomizes the classic American diner, but it has a few surprises, too — from the candlelit tables and ragtime piano music in the evening to the menu, which is full of the many admonitions your mother was so fond of ("sit up straight" and "eat all your vegetables"). The owner and the lighthearted waiters go out of their way to make families feel at home here.

Good choices for the kids are the excellent steak burgers (which you can customize with cheese and bacon), the grilled chicken and hot open-face turkey sandwiches, and the homemade round French fries. Breakfast is available all day.

Adults may find the blue plate specials appealing, as well as other diner favorites, which are executed with with gourmet flourishes. They include

135

sautéed trout, grilled tuna marinated in soy and sesame sauce, and chopped steak au poive, with mashed potatoes and salad. Avoid the bland tofu burgers. The many sandwiches include Judy's (named after the owner's wife), a combination of roasted peppers, artichoke hearts and watercress topped with melted pepperjack cheese, and Russian dressing. Among the salads, try the lightly marinated Moroccan Red Salad, in which everything (peppers, tomatoes, onions) except the olives is red. Drinks include milk, juice, sodas, shakes, malts, root beer floats, egg creams, and a full bar. For dessert, the kids can go for brownies, cake, a hot fudge sundae, or splurge on a banana split.

FLIGHT 151

151 8th Ave. (between 17th & 18th Sts.)

(229-1868

🚆 A,C,E,L to 14th St.;
1,9, to 18th St.

Hours:
Sun-Thu: 11:30 AM - 1 AM
Fri & Sat: 11:30 AM - 2 AM
Brunch:
Sat & Sun: 11:30 AM - 4 PM

▬ $

Entertainment:
Pinball machine, crayons.

Flight 151 is an easygoing neighborhood bar and restaurant with a World War I flight theme. Vintage airplane photos and advertising decorate the brick walls around the booths and tables, and on the back of the menu there is a corny account of the origin of the restaurant. The airplane motif is low-key, however, as are the patrons, who seem interested more in the game of the day on the TV sets over the bar, than in the airplane parts suspended from the clouds on the ceiling.

Even though the restaurant doesn't take reservations, there is almost never a wait, and the service is fast and attentive. Featuring good, inexpensive food, there's plenty that kids like, including milk shakes, burgers, hot dogs, BBQ chicken or ribs, pastas, meatloaf, steak, or fish and chips. Don't miss the curly French fries, which Sam loves. If you are looking for just a snack, there is a typical selection of bar-type appetizers, including nachos, chicken fingers, potato skins, and salads. The dessert selection is simple: cheesecake, apple pie, or brownies with ice cream. There is a daily fixed-price lunch special for $6.95, and on the weekends the all-you-can-eat brunch is an excellent deal.

If you decide to visit Flight 151 during the warm-weather months, try to sit at one of the front "hangar" tables. The windows open wide onto the sidewalk with a captivating view of the bustling Chelsea sidewalk.

FRIEND OF A FARMER

77 Irving Pl. (between 18th & 19th Sts.)

(477-2188

🚇 4,5,6,L,N,R to
14th St./Union Sq.

Hours:
Breakfast: Mon-Thu: 8 - 11 AM
Lunch: 11 AM - 5 PM
Dinner:
Mon-Thu: 5 - 10 PM
Fri-Sun: 5 - 11 PM
Brunch:
Sat & Sun: 10 AM - 3:30 PM

💳 $$-$$$ **Entertainment:** Yes

Friend of a Farmer is a good choice when you need to please both your kids and their grandparents. This neighborhood favorite captures the rustic charm of a New England mountain inn. Hearty country cooking is nicely complemented by the wide wood floors, decorative baskets of vegetables, fruits and dried flowers, and tin ceiling lamps, antique wallpaper, rural knickknacks and samplers. There is a warm smell in the air of country cooking and baking.

We suggest sitting upstairs, where there is a lovely fireplace and big beautiful windows overlooking Irving Place. All the tables, both upstairs and down, have large pieces of white paper on top of the handsome dark-green tablecloths. Next to the salt and pepper are little jars of crayons, so you know that kids eat here a lot.

There is often a wait at dinnertime. Once you are seated, however, the staff is quick to serve bread, drinks, and the children's food. The kids' menu consists of macaroni and cheese, PB & J, grilled cheese, and chicken with pasta, each for $5.50. These come with soda, juice, regular or chocolate milk.

Sam likes the food here because they make it quickly and they make it the way he asks — not too fussy. In fact, I've even heard one adult complain that it is too much like home cooking. For that very reason, there are many items on the menu that will appeal to kids, who can choose from five different types of chicken (including pot pie, roasted, or sautéed with red peppers), meatloaf, pork or lamb chops. The fish is also prepared nicely and Sam likes the grilled swordfish. Adults should try the sautéed salmon marinated in an artichoke/mustard vinaigrette, or the sole with capers. There is a range of appetizers, but we grown-ups usually order the daily soup or one of the simple salads. Every main dish is served with vegetables, including carrots, snowpeas, potatoes, and broccoli. Drinks include an assortment of organic juices, a number of coffees and teas, wines and beer.

Friend of a Farmer is known for their rich baked desserts. Both the apple and pecan pies are wonderful. There are also many types of muffins, and several ice creams.

HOT TOMATO

676 Sixth Ave. (at 21st St.)

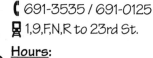

📞 691-3535 / 691-0125

🚇 1,9,F,N,R to 23rd St.

Hours:

Sun: 10 AM - 12 midnight
Mon-Wed: 11 AM - 1 AM
Thu: 11 AM - 2 AM
Fri: 11 AM - 4 AM
Sat: 10 AM - 4 AM

Brunch:

Sat & Sun: 10 AM - 4:45 PM

▬ $ **Entertainment:** No except for TVs

Hot Tomato is the perfect spot to catch your breath after bargain hunting in the Chelsea shopping district. Designed to feel like a country market restaurant, the room is decorated with plants and farm items hanging from terra cotta sponged walls with pretty ivy wallpaper. On a typical weekend, there are children at about a quarter of the tables, dining on burgers, fried chicken, turkey sandwiches with gravy, and macaroni and cheese. Other family favorites include chicken pot pie, mix-and-match pastas with a selection of sauces, and five different types of mashed potatoes. Check out the chocolate milk or one of their thick rich shakes. For dessert, your kids won't want to miss the chocolate pudding with Oreos, the ice cream sundaes, or the pecan pie.

The weekend brunch is quite popular, with classic egg dishes, buttermilk pancakes, and thick French toast with strawberries. The big homemade sticky buns are just like Granny makes, with lots of cinnamon, sugar, and pecans. Oh, and the rich hot tomato soup is pretty good too!

MAN RAY

169 8th Ave. (between 18th & 19th Sts.)

(627-4220

A,C,E,L to 14th St.;
  1,9 to 18th St.

Hours:
Lunch: Mon-Fri: 12 noon - 3 PM
Dinner:
Mon-Thu: 5:30 - 11 PM
Fri & Sat: 5:30 PM - 12 midnight
Sun: 5:30 - 11 PM

Brunch:
Sat: 11 AM - 3:30 PM
Sun: 11 AM - 4PM

$-$$ **Entertainment:** No

Located next to the Joyce Theater, Man Ray is a handsome restaurant that Sam and I like for dinner or brunch. Long and narrow, the restaurant is dominated in front by a beautiful dark wood bar. The decor has a spare, European flair with simple black granite tables, small dark-green leather booths, and sponged vanilla walls. A large reproduction of one of Man Ray's surrealist paintings hangs in the quiet rear dining room, which is where we like to sit. (The kitchen and rest rooms are located down a flight of stairs, which causes a lot of traffic in the front dining room.)

The menu features a number of items that might appeal to Sam's set including pizzas (plain cheese and tomato, grilled chicken, and eggplant, tomato, and garlic), pastas, burgers, and dishes such as a grilled half chicken with fries, fried chicken, pork chops, and grilled filet mignon with mashed potatoes, all for $9.95 to $11.95. The interesting contemporary fare also appeals to adults, and some

141

of the dishes that we have enjoyed are the seared tuna with julienned vegetables and garlic, and the sirloin pepper steak. The food is tasty and well priced, especially at brunch. There is a daily $6.95 luncheon special. Service can be a bit slow but the staff is congenial and accommodating. The tables are a little close for children under five and there is no entertainment.

MARY ANN'S

116 8th Ave. (at 16th St.)

(633-0877

🚇 A,C,E,1,2,3,9 to 14th St.;
   L to 8th Ave.

Hours:
Lunch Mon-Fri: 12 noon - 4 PM
Dinner:
Mon-Thu: 4 - 10:30 PM
Fri & Sat: 4 - 11 PM
Sun: 4 - 10 PM

Brunch:
Sat & Sun: 12 noon - 4 PM

💳 No AMEX $-$$ **Entertainment:** No

Mary Ann's, with four locations in Manhattan, is an ideal choice for good traditional Mexican fare at modest prices. With its "La Bamba" music, handmade tiles and stucco walls, punched tin star-shaped lamps, and Mexican blankets, you almost feel like you're in Tijuana. Be sure to go early — by 8:15 PM, every table will be filled and there will be a crowd at the bar waiting to eat.

First thing, Sam dives into the bottomless bowl of free chips and salsa. The homemade guacamole starter is served in a stone cornmeal grinder. The $3.95 kids' menu provides large servings of tacos, enchiladas, cheese quesadillas, chicken fajitas, or crispy flauta chicken rolls, all with rice, beans, or French fries. All the other dishes are ample, too — we never leave hungry.

The sizzling fajitas, available in steak, chicken or vegetarian variations, served with a lot of fanfare, are probably the most popular dish on the menu, but you really can't go wrong with any of the classic Mexican combination plates. We have especially enjoyed the Santa Fe sirloin burritos, the taco and enchilada specials, and the Mary Ann's combo, a shrimp burrito and chicken tostado. Vegetarian varieties are also available. For something a little different, try the camarones Veracruz, a delicious preparation of sautéed jumbo shrimp. Like most of the other dishes, these are served with generous sides of rice, beans, and salad.

Other locations:
East Village: 80 2nd Ave.
(at 5th St.) 475-5939
Upper East Side: 1503 2nd Ave.
(at 78th St.) 249-6165 (See review.)
Upper West Side: 2452 Broadway
(at 91st St.) 877-0132

MAYROSE

920 Broadway (at 21st Street)

☎ 533-3663

🚇 N,R,6 to 23rd St.

Hours:
Breakfast:
Mon-Fri: 7 - 11 AM
Lunch: 11 AM - 5 PM
Dinner:
Mon: 5 - 11 PM
Tue-Sat: 5 - 12 midnight
Sun: Closed

Brunch:
Sat: 7 AM - 5 PM
Sun: 7 AM - 4 PM

💳 $ **Entertainment:** No

Mayrose is a cross between a California-style diner and a soda fountain joint. Bustling and informal, it always seems filled with Flatiron creative types and young publishing and advertising folk. The restaurant, too, is colorful — with big comfortable green banquettes, yellow chairs, and deep blue tabletops with the red plastic glasses and ketchup bottles on them. Floor-to-ceiling windows that overlook Broadway bring in the sunlight and a view of the activity outside.

Even though breakfast service officially ends at 11AM, eggs, omelets, pancakes, French toast, and bagels with smoked salmon are available all day. Comfort foods abound, and kids can choose from burgers, hot dogs, fried chicken, macaroni and cheese, vegetable lasagna, pork chops, meatloaf, roast beef, and a turkey dinner. Also offered are mustard-roasted salmon, grilled portobello mushrooms, marinated shrimp, salads, and sandwiches, including a wonderful fresh grilled tuna on semolina bread. The bar serves beer and wine.

For dessert, load up on cheesecake, carrot cake, or ice cream sundaes, with or without the brownie. But what would a soda fountain be without root beer floats, ice cream sodas, and other classic concoctions? Sam loves the milk shakes — that's one of the reasons we come here.

PATSY'S PIZZERIA
509 3rd Ave. (at 34th St.)

(689-7500
🚇 6 to 33rd St.
Hours:
Sun-Thu: 12 noon - 11 PM
Fri & Sat: 12 noon - 12 midnight
Brunch: No

 $-$$ **Entertainment:** No

In the first quarter of this century, several young Italian pizza chefs, including John of John's Pizzeria, Tottono of Coney Island, and Patsy Lancieri, learned their craft at Gennaro Lombardi's restaurant. These chefs then went on to open their own, now famous, pizzerias. The one Patsy Lancieri opened in 1933 in East Harlem is still in business, serving not only pizza but also salads, soups, pastas, and desserts.

KIDS EAT NEW YORK

Recently, four branches of Patsy's Pizzeria have opened in Manhattan, all of which we recommend for families. The Murray Hill Patsy's is a well-lit, clean family restaurant with faux granite-topped tables, wood cafe chairs, and a copper-colored tin ceiling. The ecru walls, above the natural wood trim, are decorated with a nondescript collection of celebrity photos.

Patsy's Pizzeria offers brick-oven pizzas and an extensive menu that includes appetizers, salads, and pasta. The pizza ovens are in the dining rooms, where you can watch the chefs at work. Pizzas cost $10.95 and $12.95 and toppings are an additional $2 each. The small pizza is certainly big enough for two kids. Salads and pastas are available in individual and family-sized portions. Roughly twice the price of the generous single servings, the "big bowl" family orders are an excellent buy, easily serving a family of four.

There are 11 pastas on the menu (plus specials) ranging from pasta Bolognese to linguine with a red seafood or white clam sauce. The five salad choices are relatively traditional and include mozzarella with sundried tomatoes, as well as arugula, endive, and radicchio. The desserts are traditionally Italian. Beverage choices include sodas, beers, and Italian wines. Very casual in ambiance, the room is a little loud, so kids can be noisy. The service is fast and efficient, if a little impersonal.

Other locations: (See reviews.)
Greenwich Village: 67 University Pl.
(between 10th & 11th Sts.) 533-3500
Upper East Side: 1312 2nd Ave.
(at 69th St.) 639-1000
Upper West Side: 64 W. 74th St.
(at Columbus Ave.) 579-3000

RODEO GRILL

375 3rd Ave. (at 27th St.)

📞 683-6500

🚇 6 to 28th St.

Hours:
11:30 AM - 12 midnight
Brunch: Sat & Sun: 11 AM - 4 PM

💳 **$-$$**   **Entertainment:** Western decor

Note: **KIDS EAT FREE** Mon. nights (under 12 yrs. old; 2 per adult)

When we go to the Rodeo Grill, Sam and his buddies dress up in their cowboy boots and hats and really get into the spirit. The place is divided into two parts — a western-themed restaurant and a music bar. The restaurant is loaded with western memorabilia and artifacts, including a full-sized bison. The clientele ranges from families to yuppies stopping in on the way home from work.

The Rodeo Grill has become a popular destination for Southwestern American cuisine. We immediately order a plate of BBQ ribs for the table as soon as we arrive. We're also partial to the three-cheese quesdilla appetizer — as a starter, it is large enough for several people, as a main course, it will serve one.

The new $3.95 kids' menu of burgers, hot dogs, or chicken fingers is still in transition; Southwestern-inspired items will be added.

147

KIDS EAT NEW YORK

On Monday nights, two kids per adult can order from the children's menu meal for free.

The regular offerings include popular sizzling fajitas, which come with all the ingredients you need to roll your own; the kitchen will provide additional tortillas if you run out. The chef is particularly proud of her savory black angus rib eye steak, stuffed with garlic paste and served with roasted red potatoes. Don't overlook the dumpling-like vegetable empanadas, which are filled with grilled vegetables and manchego cheese. The cod, fried in a cornmeal crust, is accompanied by rice, beans, and salad, as are all entrees.

For dessert, we love the Apple Sopapillas (handmade puff pastries topped with apples sautéed in maple syrup) and the "Fat Elvis," a deep-fried Kahula-flavored banana chimichanga covered with chocolate. Both are served with ice cream.

TWIGS

196 8th Ave. (at 20th St.)

☎ 633-6735

🚇 C,E to 23rd St.; A to 14th St.;
1,9 to 18th St.

Hours:
Dinner: 5 PM - 12 midnight
Brunch:
Sat & Sun: 12 noon - 4 PM

💳 $-$$ **Entertainment:** No

Twigs is a busy neighborhood restaurant known for pastas, pizzas, and grilled entrees. Casual in style, it is simple and clean, with no decor to speak of. Because the tables in the middle are set close together, kids have more elbow room on the sides or the front of the room. But you don't have to worry about noisy children here — the din of the other diners' conversations masks much.

The $6.50 children's menu offers generously-sized servings of penne with meat sauce, buttered linguine, or the roasted fish of the day, which may be mahimahi with vegetables and wonderful mashed potatoes. If your family is in the mood for pizza, you have a choice of ten types, from the basic Margherita ($8.50) to the Casablanca ($10) with shrimp and eggplant in a goat cheese tomato sauce. Appetizers include escargot, mussels steamed in wine, garlic and olive oil, and Caesar salad.

Many folks come here to enjoy a big bowl of pasta. Our seafood linguine was chock-full of mussels, clams, and shrimp in a zesty red sauce ($13.75). Also delicious is the fettuccine Alfredo with wild

149

mushrooms, peas and bacon ($12.75). Among the grilled meats, a basic grilled chicken and a delightful Turkish chicken paillard served over couscous with yougurt (both $10.75) stand out. The grilled shell steak ($13.95) is nicely complemented with sweet sauteed onions and those memorable mashed potatoes.

WORLD ROOM
(at Coffee Shop)
29 Union Square W.
(at 16th Street, located behind the Coffee Shop)

(243-7969

N,R,L,4,5,6 to Union Sq.

Hours:
Lunch: 12 noon - 5 PM
Dinner: 6 PM - 12 midnight
Brunch: Sat & Sun: 9 AM - 5 PM

$$ **Entertainment:** Crayons & coloring placemats.

 6+

Behind the famed hip hangout Coffee Shop is a secret called World Room. Not a restaurant for all kids, if you have a sophisticated crew of youngsters ready for a stylish experience, this is a novel place to go for lunch or early dinner.

The decor is "cosmopolitan" — a suave late fifties/early sixties take-off featuring bright colors and chrome accents which, combined with the dimmed lighting, creates an appealing rather than overbearing effect. There's a lot of activity, and jazz in the foreground, so there's no fear of being too loud. The staff is young and energetic. Bring crayons, as the paper-covered tables are ideal for drawing.

Gourmet pizza is a World Room specialty, with "pizza bar" seating so that you can watch the preparation and the baking. Although there isn't a children's menu, kids have plenty of choices — chicken, including grilled or roasted, as well as an assortment of burgers.

Adults will find interesting dishes including rack of lamb, seared tuna, calamari, lobster, osso bucco, sashimi, oysters, goat cheese salad, and several wok combinations. Deserts include crème brûlée, chocolate mocha mousse, and pear tarte Tatin. There is a full bar, plus wine list, sodas, tea and coffee.

CHELSEA PIERS SPORTS AND ENTERTAINMENT CENTER

W. 23rd St. and the Hudson River

••••••••••••••••••••••••••••••••

(General Information: 336-6666

TRANSPORTATION:

🚇 Most major lines connect with the 23rd Street M23 crosstown bus.

Free bus:
NY Waterway provides a complimentary bus or jitney service that runs every ten to 15 minutes along 12th Avenue from the World Trade Center to 38th Street. All are painted bright red, white, and blue and have huge "W" signs on the sides. NY Waterway is printed on the front windshields in large letters. You can hail the buses (just as you would hail a taxi), anywhere along 12th Avenue, and you can take the bus from Chelsea Piers to anywhere along its route.

Parking: On-site, parking is available. Fee.

Taxis: Generally available at Chelsea Piers.

Chelsea Piers offers many sports and fitness facilities that are open to children, including:

Skyrink: Year-round ice skating

Golf Club: Multi-story driving range

Roller Rinks: Rollerskating, rollerblading, & hockey (Skate rentals are available.)

In the Field House:
Gymnastics
Rock climbing
Indoor soccer
Karate classes
Lacrosse and field hockey
Basketball courts
Batting cages
Summer sports camp

Lessons are available at all these facilities.
Call for details, including fees.

Chelsea Piers also features a terrific waterfront esplanade and park and a pleasure boat marina. On Pier 60 is the Chelsea Piers Sports Center, a private health club not open to children under 16. Silver Screen Studios, at the back of the complex, includes six television and movie production sound stages not open to the general public.

THE CHELSEA BREWING COMPANY RESTAURANT
Chelsea Piers, Pier 59

(336-6440

Hours:
12 noon- 1 or 2 AM
(kitchen closes at 11 PM)
Brunch: No

$-$$ **Entertainment:**
Chelsea Piers; the view

Note: Kids' menu Saturday & Sunday daytime only; Reservations not available for outdoor patio.

This handsome eatery overlooks the pleasure boat marina and the side of the driving range. The multilevel dining facility has booths and tables inside and an outdoor cafe next to the boat slips. All levels have excellent water views. The ceiling is very high, with warehouse-type exposed duct work, brick floors, and attractive old-fashioned globe "street lamps." At the bar are several enormous vats containing the six specialty beers and ales (the Raspberry Wheat Ale is excellent) that are brewed on location.

KIDS EAT NEW YORK

The large menu features pizzas that range from the simple Margarita to the spicy Southwestern, made with ground beef and jalapenos, and the Chelsea, which has sun-dried tomatoes, black olives, and red and green peppers. All are prepared in the brick oven adjacent to the dining room. Kids might also wish to order one of the burgers or a sandwich such as grilled chicken breast on a roll, hot roast beef, tuna melt, or grilled cheese. The burgers, and many entrees such as pork chops, steak, and fish, are grilled on the patio. In addition, there are salads (try the grilled vegetable salad with zucchini, eggplant, and endive over greens) and pastas like fettucine in a fresh tomato sauce and rigatoni with broccoli, sun-dried tomatoes, and a nice touch of Moroccan olives. The food is tasty, though not outstanding, and most dishes are priced from $7 to $10 with entrees costing $12 to $15. Desserts include cakes and pies, and beverages include milk, fresh squeezed juices, sodas, coffee, tea, and a full bar. Unfortunately the service is extremely slow, and you may have to be aggressive if you want to be waited on promptly.

CHOCK FULL O' NUTS

Chelsea Piers, Pier 60

☏ 336-6454

Hours:
8 AM - 8 PM
Brunch: No

💳 $ **Entertainment:** Chelsea Piers

Note: Restrooms are public access

This small, handsome take-out cafe with plain black modern tables and bentwood chairs has an inside seating area and a sheltered outside counter that overlooks the charter boat slips. There is no table service. A good choice for an easy, inexpensive snack or lunch, the menu has pizzas by the slice (a large slice is $1.99 to $2.99 depending on the toppings), and sandwiches such as roast beef, turkey, ham, or tuna salad, all with lettuce and tomato, for $4.95. The kitchen will make grilled cheese for kids as a special order. I like the mozzarella and tomato on foccacia with pesto sauce, and the slightly spicy marinated southwestern chicken sandwich with peppers and onions in a pita pouch. Soups change daily and include Manhattan clam chowder, corn chowder, and crab bisque. The small $2.50 size is plenty big enough for us. Bakery snacks include cookies, muffins, brownies, and coffee cake; Haagen- Dazs bars and soft frozen yogurt are available. Beverages include sport drinks, OJ, sodas, ice tea, lemonade, and of course, Chock Full o' Nuts coffee.

THE CRAB HOUSE

Chelsea Piers — at the end of Pier 61

(366-4111

Hours:

Summer Hours:
Mon-Thu: 11:30 AM - 11 PM
Fri: 11:30 AM - 12 midnight
Sat: 12 noon - 12 midnight
Sun: 12 noon - 11 PM

Winter Hours:
Mon-Thu: 4 - 10 PM
Fri & Sat:
   11:30 AM - 12 midnight
Sun: 12 noon - 10 PM

Brunch: No

 $$-$$$ **Entertainment:** Yes

The Crab House has great Hudson River views on three sides. The decorations are terrific and interesting to kids starting with the large statue outside of a King Kong-sized giant crab perched on top of a replica of the Empire State Building. Inside there are oversized tropical fish models hanging everywhere and nice versions of buoys, anchors, fish nets, etc., that typically adorn seafood eateries. This spacious restaurant can seat at least 300 at its large brown paper-covered tables and booths. The place is pretty noisy, so loud toddlers aren't a problem. The best place to sit is at the pier end of the restaurant or in season, on the patio. These tables are worth the wait, not only for the water view but because from your seat you can also watch the kids play on the outside promenade. The service is very slow (we had to be demanding) and you may have to ask for the $3.99 kids' menu, which offers a choice of fried chicken, shrimp, fish and chips or a combo meal. All come with fries and a mushy fruit salad. Shakes, nonalcoholic pina coladas and sundaes for kids are $1.95. The menu sheet itself has some good activities on it and comes complete with a little net bag of crayons, stickers, and a toy.

The Crab House is part of a Florida-based chain. The adult menu features a wide variety of seafood appetizers and chowders; a large selection of fresh fish (including mahimahi, red snapper, and rainbow trout) that can be grilled, fried, or broiled; crabs, including Maryland Blue, Alaskan Snow, and king; lobster; and steak or prime rib. The seafood has always been fresh, but somewhat uninspired, and our hot dishes have always arrived cold. Some of the best selections are the raw shrimp, oysters, and littleneck clams, the red Bahamian conch chowder, and the plain grilled swordfish and tuna steaks. The very good Chesapeake Crab Sampler includes a jumbo crab-cake, a plain sautéed softshell crab, a few deep-fried oysters, coleslaw, and fries.

Nearby restaurants you might want to consider as part of your Chelsea Piers outing:
EMPIRE DINER 210 10th Ave.
(at 22nd St.) 243-2736
BENDIX DINER 219-221 8th Ave.
(at 21st St.) 366-0560
CHELSEA GRILL 135 8th Ave.
(between 16th & 17th Sts.) 929-9766
EIGHTEENTH & EIGHTH 159 8th Ave.
(at 18th St.) 242-5000
FLIGHT 151 151 8th Ave.
(between 17th & 18th Sts.) 229-1868
HOT TOMATO 676 Sixth Ave.
(at 21st St.) 691-3535

MIDTOWN

• • • • • • • • • • • • • • • •

For the purposes of this book, we are defining **Midtown** as the section of Manhattan that runs from 34th Street to 59th Street, from the Hudson River to the East River. This area also includes the theater district.

RESTAURANTS
• •

ATTRACTIONS with RESTAURANTS

ALL STAR CAFE, OFFICIAL
1540 Broadway(at 45th Street)

📞 840-8326

🚇 1,2,3,7,9,N,R,S to Times Sq.

Hours:
Lunch/Dinner: 11 AM - 2 AM
Brunch: No

 No AMEX $$ **Entertainment::** Yes

The sports-themed All Star Cafe is jointly owned by several super-star athletes including Andre Agassi, Joe Montana, Shaquille O'Neal, and Wayne Gretzky, as well as the Planet Hollywood group. Located on the third floor, you will be cheerfully directed up a series of ramps, escalators and elevators to the maitre'd stand. (Unfortunately, at each of these levels, you will be confronted with a large souvenir stand.) While the restaurant is spread out over two levels, the main dining room is the best place to be seated.

No expense was spared in the decorations. The circular main dining room is set up like a mini sports arena, complete with a central multimedia scoreboard display, huge video screens, and a Budweiser blimp that soars about the ceiling. Underneath the scoreboard is a circular bar surrounded by several rows of tables and a circular row of "really cool" large baseball-mitt-shaped booths. To the side is a second dining room that features an enormous video screen; up the wide metal stadium-type stairs are additional dining areas with tables that overlook the activities below. Sports memorabilia is everywhere.

The waiters are very friendly (diners are referred to as "players" here), but unfortunately the service is very slow. Although the $4.95 children's menu only offers grilled cheese with fries or pasta marinara, there is no problem finding additional things to order from the main menu, such as burgers, hot dogs, sandwiches, salads, fried chicken, steak, and ribs. The food is only OK, and overpriced, but the main menu portions are huge, so kids can split their orders. Desserts are large and caloric — with the cheesecake, the choco-late-chip-cookie sundae, and the apple pie as high-lights. Milk, shakes, malts, sodas and specialty drinks (with and without alcohol), are some of the beverage options, but watch out — the waiter will give a sales pitch to the kids to buy a souvenir glass or sports bottle (and after we decided to go ahead and buy one, the items were out of stock, every time we visited).

The activity level is frenetic, from game replays being shown on the countless video monitors, to the non-stop overhead announcements that can barely be understood over the blare of rock music, to the frenzied traffic of the waiters. Sports activities, such as a basketball shoot outs, are occasionally organized, but this was a source of frustration for our kids as the staff only selected three or four kids to participate and while they promise to repeat it every hour, they often don't.

BENIHANA OF TOKYO

120 E. 56th St. (between Lexington & Park Aves.)

☏ 593-1627

🚇 E,F to 53rd St./5th Ave.

Hours:

BENIHANA OF TOKYO

47 W. 56th St. (between 5th & 6th Aves.)

☏ 581-0930

🚇 B,Q,N,R to 57th St.

Hours:
Lunch:
Mon-Fri: 11:30 AM - 2:30 PM
Sat: 12:30 AM- 2:30 PM
Sun: 1 - 4 PM

Dinner:
Mon-Thu: 5:30 - 10:30 PM
Fri-Sat: 5:30 - 11:30 PM
Sun: 4 - 10 PM

Brunch: No

💳 $$-$$$ **Entertainment:** Japanese chefs cook at your table

Note: No kids' menu but kids can split an adult portion.

Benihana is great for a special treat or to celebrate an important occasion. The food is good, and it is a lot of fun watching it being prepared. You are escorted to a seat at a grill table that typically accommodates seven diners arranged on three sides; the fourth is reserved for the Japanese chef. If your party is fewer than six people, the restaurant may seat you with another group. Most of the table area is the hot grill; your plates will remain at the warm edge throughout the meal, while drinks sit on a narrow wooden counter. The dining room is decorated in a simple Japanese style with pottery, masks, and carvings. Benihana, which is named after a Japanese flower, is a national chain founded by Rocky Aoki, a race car driver and a hot air balloonist.

Before you order, you will be handed a hot towel to clean your hands. At the two Manhattan locations there is no separate children's menu, which makes for an expensive night out. Sam loves the food here — he raves about the steak dinners, which are $17 to 18.50, depending on the cut. The chicken dinner is $14 and there are also deluxe combinations including steak and lobster. All the dinners come with soup, salad, shrimp appetizer, vegetables, and rice. At lunch the prices are about half as much, and entrees come with salad, vegetables and rice. Sodas are topped with little paper parasols, and there is a full bar including Japanese beers and wine. The only desserts are fruit and ice creams in exotic flavors.

The chefs are all very friendly to kids and will carry on quite a conversation with them if they are not too shy. Kids love watching them slice and dice, and if you are lucky enough to get a really skilled chef, there may be some food acrobatics. Sam likes to show off his chopstick skills here, but forks are also available for backup. If you celebrate a birthday at Benihana, you get a small fruit platter with a Buddha centerpiece and everyone gets to pose with the Buddha for a Polaroid while the staff sings the Japanese version of "Happy Birthday."

BROOKLYN DINER

212 W. 57th St. (between 7th Ave. & Broadway)

(Reservations: 581-8900
977-1957, 977-2280

🚇 N,R to 57th St.

Hours:
Mon-Thu: 8 AM - 12 midnight
Fri/Sat: 8 AM - 1 AM
Sun: 8 AM - 11 PM
Breakfast avail. daily: 8 AM - 4 PM, 10 PM to closing.
Brunch: Sat/Sun: 8 - 11:30 AM

▬ $$ **Entertainment:** No

Note: Reservations accepted for parties of five or less only.

Located in the midst of theme-restaurant row, the Brooklyn Diner takes comfort food to new heights, but be prepared to pay for it: the prices are very much 57th Street. As you step into what looks like a classy 1940s railroad car, the first thing you may notice is the enticing smells wafting from the partially exposed kitchen. Or maybe it's the tempting desserts in the pie case immediately in front of you. There is a large mural of Ebbets Field on one wall and great windows that face 57th Street on the other. The tables are paper-covered at the banquettes and at the booths, many of which have small brass plaques identifying local celebrities, such as Paul Schafer (of the Late Night Orchestra), that dine here. The diner seats 75 to 80 and there usually isn't a wait.

The eclectic menu reflects the Brooklyn melting pot — in other words, a combination of Italian, Jewish, Spanish, German, Irish and other

164

favorites. We recommend the 15-bite hot dog, the Hungarian goulash with spaetzle, the meat-loaf made with spinach and pine nuts and served with mashed potatoes, and the sesame chicken salad, prepared with bok choy, and rice noodles. Most families will also be happy ordering the burger or BBQ chicken sandwich, as well as the daily seafood specials like grilled swordfish or salmon.

Beverage options include all the regulars plus shakes and a nice selection of wines by the glass. And don't forget dessert, which features a "strawberry blond" cheesecake with chocolate sauce, as well as fruit tarts, lemon meringue pie, and chocolate "blackout" cake. Despite the $10 minimum per person and steep prices, we love the good service and jazzy low-key atmosphere at this diner with class.

BRYANT PARK CAFE
Bryant Park at 42nd St.
(between 5th & 6th Aves.)

☎ 575-0733
🚇 B,D,F,Q to 42nd St.

Open from April to October

Hours:
(Weather Permitting)
1:30 AM to 11 PM or 12 midnight
Brunch: No

💳 $$ **Entertainment:** The park

Note: Rest rooms are in the park (public access)

Perched on the northeastern corner of Bryant Park, this is a nice place to catch your breath and unwind in midtown. Dappled sunlight filters through the high canopy of ivy-covered trees, and even on the hottest days, a nice breeze drifts in from the park. Bryant Park, which is literally the backyard of the main branch of the New York Public Library, has been the focus of several beautification projects in the last few years, and is both well-used and well-tended. With the long marble rear facade of the library as a backdrop, the skyscrapers surrounding the park provide a unique urban contrast to the park's green lawns and lush flower gardens. Often during the spring and summer, musicians and comedians provide free entertainment at the park's western end, which is both far enough away not to disrupt your meal and — as the cafe is slightly elevated — well within your view should your family choose to watch.

The Bryant Park Cafe is completely outdoors. Two large green-and-white striped canvas tents shelter both the bar and kitchen areas and over-sized market umbrellas are strategically placed among the cafe tables and rattan chairs. Planters overflowing with flowers border the cafe.

Service is friendly and attentive, but the food is pricey for a cafe. (You are paying for the setting.) The menu is New American with the focus on salads and gourmet sandwiches. And while there isn't a children's menu, there are several kid-friendly choices, including burgers, sandwiches, and chicken nuggets. The desserts include ice creams, brownie combos, tortes, and fresh fruit.

Next to the cafe, on the other side of the commemorative arch, is the Bryant Park Grill. While this is a tempting place to dine, we do not recommend it, as it is quite formal and many kids will find the food too sophisticated.

Located on the western end of the park, however, are two kiosks with carry-out food that we suggest. One specializes in focaccia sandwiches and the other in pastas, salads, soups, and sandwiches. Both are quite reasonably priced and offer beverages, as well as desserts such as Haagen-Dazs ice cream bars. There are a few cafe tables near the kiosks, as well as a large quantity of lawn chairs spread out on the grass. The park's many benches are also a good place to eat, whether you buy your food at one of the kiosks or bring your own picnic.

CAFE UN DEUX TROIS
123 W. 44th Street
(between Broadway & 6th Aves.)

354-4148

N,R,S,1,2,3,7,9,A,C,E
to 42nd St./Times Sq.

Hours:
Lunch: 12 noon - 4 PM
Dinner: 4 PM - 12 midnight
Brunch: No

$$-$$$ **Entertainment:** No

Note: Wheelchair access up a few steps

For one family we know, it is a tradition to dine at cafe un deux trois when taking in a Broadway show or movie at Times Square. A large, very French bistro, with soaring ceilings (painted with cloudscapes), sparkling chandeliers, glamorous red drapes, and pots of very big palm trees, multilingual conversations fill the air. The atmosphere may seem frenzied, and service can be distracted, but the waiters are very experienced and excellent with families.

Go before 7 PM and you will quickly be seated at a table covered with butcher paper over linens and supplied with a jar of crayons and a basket of French bread. Sam favors the traditional steak frites, a substantial grilled sirloin with fabulous French fries. We also like the roasted chicken with mushrooms and the grilled tuna over mesclun. For kids who love onion soup, the one here will be a big hit, with lots of stringy melted cheese.

Specials such as the buttery lobster bisque and the mussels in white wine sauce and garlic are listed, French style, on the mirrors. The food is consistently good, although some find it a little too salty.

The dessert menu is filled with traditional French choices such as crème caramel drowning in syrup, rich chocolate mousse, chocolate gateau, sweet apple tart and Sam's favorite, profiteroles — ice-cream-filled puff pastry covered with chocolate syrup.

CHURRASCARIA PLATAFORMA

316 W. 49th St. (between 8th & 9th Aves.)

☎ 245-0505
🚆 C,E,1,9 to 50th St.

Hours:
12 noon - 12 midnight
Brunch: No

💳 **$$$**   **Entertainment:**
Thu-Sun: from 8 PM- jazz singer

Note: **Reservations are a must** (Only accepted 24 hours in advance). Otherwise, expect a wait of 30 to 60 minutes; **All-you-can-eat:** $27 (not inc. drinks & dessert) and Monday-Thursday: Kids under 9: $14.50.

Rodizio barbecue originated in Brazil in the 1960s and has had a turn as a culinary craze in New York. All-you-can-eat feasting is the concept here. When you are seated, you are given red-and-green-sided discs instead of menus. Leave the green side up, and an unending parade of waiters bearing enormous skewers of 15 types of freshly barbecued meats will stop at your table. The ribs, steak and chicken sausage are carved directly onto your plate. Served from a cart, grilled salmon with caper sauce is also offered. Nead a break? Just turn the disc over with the red side up. And don't just stay at your table ... There is a huge double-sided buffet and salad bar that you won't want to miss.

Pots of delicious paellas, octopus salad, and South American fish stews simmer at the ends. In between is an array of cold meats, carpaccio, vegetables and salads, overseen by a lovely Brazilian lady who will gladly explain any dish.

When you return to your table, you will find an assortment of side dishes has been served. There are French fries for the kids, plus items such as fried yucca, fried plantains, and some dishes whose ingredients we could only guess at. And when you think that you can't eat another bite, the dessert cart is rolled by. We have to admit it, though, we were just too stuffed to try anything.

Churrascaria Plataforma stands out from the other *riodizios* we have tried in that it genuinely welcomes children. If a particular meat was a big hit with the kids at our table, the waiters went out of their way to return with more. The restaurant is grand in style, with a postmodern decor and generous amounts of marble and verdigris wrought iron in the front bar area. The mood is boisterous and exciting; beginning around 8 PM, Thursday through Sunday, piano cabaret music adds to the festive atmosphere.

COMFORT DINER

214 E. 45th Street (between 2nd & 3rd Aves.)

(867-4555

🚇 S,4,5,6,7 to Grand Central

<u>Hours:</u>

Breakfast: Mon-Fri: 7:30 - 10 AM

Lunch: 11 AM - 5 PM

Dinner:

Mon-Fri: 5 - 10 PM

Sat : 4 - 10 PM

Sun : 4 - 9 PM

Brunch: Sat & Sun: 9 AM - 4 PM

 $$ **Entertainment:** Color the menu

June Cleaver would have loved the Comfort Diner. Totally unassuming from the street, it is pretty as pie inside, with a turquoise, gold, and maple color scheme, lots of aluminum, stainless steel, and Formica, and multicolored tiles on the floor. You can choose to sit at a booth, a banquette or at the soda counter. The wait staff wears custom Comfort Diner bowling shirts, and the walls are decorated with Betty Crocker/Good Housekeeping 1950s colorized pictures of the ideal American family.

The people who work here are friendly to kids and you will see a lot of them, including infants in strollers. The $2.95 kids' menu offers grilled cheese, burgers, PB&J, chicken breast, macaroni and cheese, tuna fish, or a hot dog and beans. All these come with milk, juice, or soda, and (except for the pastas), include fries. There are crayons on the table to color the menu, which also includes a few jokes and activities. And if your kids have behaved themselves, they'll be invited to join the "Good Eaters' Club," whose members get to select a free toy from the grab bag.

The main menu features an inexpensive selection of basic diner comfort food — soups, salads, sandwiches, and a few surprises such as clam fritters, wild mushroom potato pancakes, southwestern chicken pot pie (with corn, black beans, and jalapenos in a cheddar spoon-bread crust), and seared salmon with watercress. There are also daily specials including pastas and desserts. There is a weekend brunch, and there are weekday breakfast specials from 7 to 10 AM.

ELLEN'S STARDUST DINER
1650 Broadway (at W. 51st St.)

☎ 956-5151

🚇 1,9, to 50th St.;
   N,R, to 49th St./7th Ave.

Hours:
Breakfast: 7:30 - 11:30 AM
Lunch/Dinner:
Sun-Thu: 11:30 PM - 12 midnight
Fri & Sat: 11:30 AM - 1 AM

Brunch:
Sat & Sun: 11:30 AM - 4:30 PM

▬ $-$$ Entertainment: Yes

If you are in the theater district, this is an absolutely great place to take the kids. Ellen Hart, the owner, was Miss Subways of 1959, and this honor has inspired the decor of this 1950s theme restaurant. The front of the restaurant features a full-sized red subway car, and inside, a soda fountain and a model subway train. You'll see lots of red or sparkling turquoise vinyl with silvery steel and aluminum. Everything, in fact, is strictly fifties — from the framed magazine advertisements, to the TV show posters, to the "Predicta" brand black-and-white television sets featuring shows such as American Bandstand that highlight Teen Angel-era recording stars.

All the waiters and waitresses have names straight out of the fifties, and boy, do they love kids! Diner favorites like burgers, hot dogs, chicken fingers, sandwiches, and steak are the standouts. In addition there are a range of salads, omelets, sandwiches, and grilled or Tex-Mex entrees, including both seafood and vegetarian options. Beverages include milk, juice, coffee, wine, beer (including microbrews), and soda fountain classics (Sam's milk shake arrived with an 18-inch straw). The dessert menu is extensive.

On weekend evenings, variety shows — Elvis, Abbott & Costello, Comedy, etc. — are often scheduled. There are also singing waiters, from 7 to 10 PM, Thursday through Sunday, who are a lot of fun (and even at other times, they will usually honor a child's request to sing).

FASHION CAFE
51 Rockefeller Plaza
(on 51st St. between 5th & 6th Aves.)

☎ 765-3131

🚇 B,D,F,Q to Rockefeller Center; N,R to 49th St.; 1,9 to 50th St.

Hours:
11:30 AM - 1 AM
Brunch: No

 $$ **Entertainment:** Yes

Want a great place to take the girls for a special treat? Try this mega-example of restaurant marketing, fronted by the fabulous foursome of supermodels — Elle McPherson, Claudia Schiffer, Naomi Campbell, and Christy Turlington. Not that there is any chance you'll see them, unless you count watching them in the nonstop videos that are shown on the many monitors throughout the restaurant. And even though this place is really a mausoleum to fashion, kids don't see the flaws. They love the glass cases filled with glam rags, the star-patterned catwalk and a ceiling with clouds and lit-up stars. Be sure to look for the 3-D mural of New York on the center wall and the wacky mirrors in the rest rooms. The dining room is set up in a circle with an assortment of individual tables, booths, and banquettes on various levels. An odd blend of movie tunes, classic rock, R & B, and club music is pumped in over the sound system.

Everything is for sale here, including the menu (at $8.95). So adults, relax, and accept the fact that you are going to be subjected to tacky displays, videos of last year's runway shows, slightly expensive, mediocre food and slow service in a totally tourist environment. Remember, you're here for the kids.

Grilled cheese and kids' portions of pasta (both for $4.95) are available, but you have to ask for them (they're not on the menu and the waiters will not voluntarily let you know about them). The main menu itself is quite nicely designed in the shape of a camera and is decorated with pictures of jewelry, film canisters, and beauty aids. Appetizers include grilled shrimp or spring rolls, salads, sandwiches, pizzas, pastas, and entrees. Grilled vegetable, Cobb, and Caesar salads are priced from $8.95 to $10.95. Sandwiches are in the price range of the salads, and there are soup and salad or sandwich specials for $8 to $9. The pastas and entrees ($10.95 to $17.95) include penne with chicken, broccoli and sundried tomatoes in a white wine sauce, bowtie pasta with salmon and peas, and entrees such as steak, veal chops, chicken, and fish. We did think that it was odd that there's nothing on the menu that a fashion model would eat, especially the range of very fattening dessert like Oreo cheesecake, brownies with ice cream, three-berry tarts, tiramisu, shakes and malts.

Service can be very friendly but it can be quite slow, too. One of our orders took forever, arrived cold and not the way we ordered it, but we decided to grin and bear it, rather than wait again for the food to be remade.

HAMBURGER HARRY'S

145 W. 45th St. (between 6th & 7th Ave.)

(840-2756

1,9,2,3,N,R,5,7 to Times Sq.

Hours:
Mon-Sat: 11:30 AM - 11:30 PM
Sun: Closed
Brunch: No

 $

Entertainment: Crayons and coloring sheets.

     5+

There are two Hamburger Harry's, once both owned by the same person. Today they are owned and run separately and have different but similar menus. Both locations are good places to take kids.

From the street, this restaurant may not look like very much, but the midtown Hamburger Harry's is more than just a burger joint.

KIDS EAT NEW YORK

Besides the 18 types of mesquite-grilled hamburgers, they offer grilled chicken, steaks, and fish as well as daily specials. Menu options also include soups, salads, sandwiches, chili, burritos, and fajitas. Prices are low, and because Harry's is located in the theater district, they understand the need for fast service.

Be sure to ask for the children's menu and crayons. (The waiters are not so good about automatically handing them out.) Kid-sized burgers, tuna boats, pizza muffins, and footlong hot dogs, all with fries, are $4.99, and there are a few simple games on the menu for kids to play. They serve up a big milkshake for $3.95, as well as milk, sodas; there is a full bar. For dessert there are key lime, apple, blueberry or pecan pies, hot fudge sundaes, and cheesecake.

The restaurant is long and narrow, with wooden cafe chairs and tables on several levels. There are TVs over the bar, a jukebox in the back, and the walls are decorated with mirrors and photos of Broadway stars. The ambiance is a jolly mix of families, seniors, pre-theater goers, and midtown professional types, with the dress ranging from suits to jeans. Kids can be a little boisterous here and no one will get upset — this is not a hushed dining room type of place. So if you find yourself in the theater district, and hungry, try Harry's for a good basic meal.

HARD ROCK CAFE

221 W. 57th St. (between Broadway & 7th Ave.)

☎ 459-9320

🚇 N,R,B,Q to 57th St.;
   D,E,B to 7th Ave.

Hours:
Sun-Thu: 11:30 AM - 12:30 PM
Fri & Sat: 11:30 AM - 1:30 AM
Brunch: No

 💳 $-$$ **Entertainment:** Yes

      20+

Twenty-five years old and still going strong, the Hard Rock Cafe is the granddaddy of theme restaurants. The first Hard Rock opened in London in 1971 as a place to get real American burgers. Los Angeles is home to HR No. 2, and in 1984, New York's own, the first to display rock n' roll memorabilia, opened. The restaurant is spread over two levels; the large second-floor balcony overlooks the much larger dining room below and a stage that doubles as a dining area when there are no scheduled shows. Tucked underneath the balcony is a guitar-shaped bar that is really a holding area for customers waiting for their tables. Rock music, of course, plays loudly on the sound system, and music videos and interviews are shown on monitors throughout the restaurant.

Because of the recent proliferation of theme restaurants in the 57th Street area, the wait here is shorter than it used to be. Plan on 15 minutes for a summer weekday lunch, longer in the evenings, and much longer on the weekends.

KIDS EAT NEW YORK

There is a host just inside the front door who will take your name and page you when your table is ready. If the wait is long, you'll be lined up outside on the sidewalk, behind velvet ropes. All of your party must be present to be seated.

Contrary to what you may expect, the prices are only a little bit higher than they should be. The best plan is to order one of the burgers, which come with fries, or one of the large salads, because for $7 to $10, plus the cost of a beverage, you can enjoy the entire Hard Rock experience without breaking the bank. Sam prefers the bacon cheeseburger (a Hard Rock classic). My favorite salad is the South of the Border, which comes with lettuce, guacamole, taco chips and either chicken or chili. BBQ ribs, fish, strip steak, and fajitas are more expensive entrees. The "Lil' Rock" children's menu book, with rock puns and coloring activities, was added last year. All the kids' faves — burgers, dogs, PB&J, grilled cheese, and chicken tenders — are now available for $5.99 with fries and juice, soda, or milk. Sam recommends their shakes and floats. The desserts are a big hit with kids and anyone not on a diet — sundaes, banana splits, and brownies with ice cream and hot fudge.

The Hard Rock Cafe is full of rock n' roll memorabilia, which is its main draw. The Beatles, the Grateful Dead, the Rolling Stones, Jimi Hendrix, Elvis Presley and Michael Jackson are just a few of the musical legends whose photographs, guitars, clothing, and gold records are on display. Kids of all ages love to wander around here looking at everything, so be sure to ask your waiter for the location guide to all the memorabilia — it's free, you can take it home with you, and it provides interesting details about many of the items.

HARLEY DAVIDSON CAFE
1370 6th Ave. (at 56th St.)

☎ 245-6000
🚇 N,R to 57th St.;
 B,D,E to 7th Ave.;
 B,Q to 57th St.

Hours:
11:30 AM - 2 AM
Brunch: No

 $-$$

Entertainment: Photo session; On the weekends there are face painters, temporary tattoo artists, a caricaturist, and an Elvis impersonator.

Note: Reservations taken for weekdays only; must be made that week.

Perfect for kids, the Harley Davidson Cafe is a squeaky-clean version of motorcycle mania. There are impeccable Harleys everywhere you turn — starting with the one parked right outside and another over the front entrance. The motorcycle motif continues inside with memorabilia all over the place: floor-to-ceiling pictures of Harley-owning movie and rock stars, autographed guitars from Harley owners (including one from Bob Dylan), gold records from Harley riders like Bon Jovi, and a scarf once owned by Elvis. The light fixtures are made of motorcycle parts — fenders, engines, headlights — and machine shop grating is used extensively in the decor.

The first floor features a bar (with a Harley pinball machine) and a large dining room with a two-story-high ceiling dominated by a huge American

181

flag. Downstairs are several smaller dining rooms, the rest rooms (including a baby changing station), a wall listing the names of stars that are Harley owners, and an area where kids can have photos taken while "riding" a Harley. While you wait to be seated, don't be surprised if you feel the wind and rumble of motorcycles. And waiting is definitely part of the experience here — the lines can resemble those for theme park attractions if you haven't made a reservation or if you go at peak times.

Once you are seated, though, you will find the service cheerful and efficient. Although there isn't a separate children's menu, the kitchen is set up for kids and will prepare kids' portions. Macaroni and cheese, small burgers, and grilled cheese sandwiches are on the menu, which lists additional pastas and burgers (including turkey burgers), BBQ, roasted chicken, vegetarian chili, sloppy joes, and club sandwiches, swordfish, salmon, crab cakes, and steak. Milk, sodas, and coffees are available; there is also a full bar. Desserts are of the hi-cal variety, ranging from Mississippi mud pie and peanut butter pie to cheesecake, sundaes and brownie ice cream sandwiches. The back of the menu is not to be missed as it is full of information highlighting the 90 years of Harley Davidson motorcycles and culture.

Sam loves this restaurant. He calls it "the best, really cool, and awesome!" This is the original Harley Davidson Cafe (soon to be a chain), having opened its doors in October of 1993. We highly recommend that you give it a whirl, but watch out for those lines.

HUDSON PLACE
538-540 3rd Ave. (at 36th St.)

☎ 686-6660

🚇 6 to 33rd St.

Hours:
Lunch/Dinner:
Mon-Thu: 11:30 AM - 11 PM
Fri: 11:30 AM - 12 midnight
Sat: 12 noon - 12 midnight
Sun: 12 noon - 10 PM

Brunch: Sat & Sun 12 noon - 3 PM

💳 $-$$ **Entertainment:** No

Note: Reservations for lunch only

The big open dining room at Hudson Place features photos of old Hudson River cruiseliners and Deco steamship posters. Comfortable bistro chairs are set around the large, well-spaced dining tables, covered with tablecloths and butcher paper, and there are crayons set out on each table. To the side of this large dining room there are big handsome booths near the bar, and a rear dining room decorated as a library. In season, windows open up onto Third Avenue.

The menu offers lots of kid-friendly food choices and Sam suggests either the ten-inch pan pizzas, or grilled specialties such as steak or turkey burgers, chicken on skewers, or tuna steak. Other entrees include BBQ ribs and steak sandwiches. Pasta is emphasized here, and kids can order a side dish of spaghetti with butter or marinara sauce for $4. Grownups will enjoy the spaghetti carbonara, served in a light cream sauce that includes peas and mushrooms, the seafood linguine (with mussels, shrimp, scallops, calamari and roasted garlic), or the spicy shrimp pasta diablo. Portions are generous and

183

prices low, the most expensive entree the 14 oz. grilled sirloin at $14.95. The restaurant is very clean, and the staff goes out of its way to be nice and friendly to kids. While many diners dress in suits, casual attire is also appropriate.

INAGIKU

111 E. 49th St. (between Park & Lexington Aves.)

(355-0440

🚇 6 to 51st St.

Hours:
Lunch, Mon-Fri: 12 noon - 2 PM
Dinner, daily: 5:30 AM - 10 PM
Brunch: No

▬ **$$$-$$$$** **Entertainment:** No

Note: Reservations necessary

Inagiku is a sophisticated Japanese restaurant that combines traditional ceremonial elements with modern cuisine. Located in the Waldorf-Astoria, but with its own entrance on 49th Street, the restaurant recently underwent a million-dollar renovation resulting in a spare and beautiful interior designed by Adam Tihany. The tables are of varied natural woods with simple cushioned armchairs or banquette seating with a ying/yang motif woven in the upholstery. Abstract interpretations of grains of rice are sculpted into the light fixtures. Curved slatted wood walls and frosted glass dividers subtly break up the room. Other than conversations, there is only a twinkle of background music.

184

Quite expensive and inappropriate for younger children, Inagiku should be reserved for a very special occasion. The food and service are extraordinary. Sam was fascinated with our waitress's traditional Japanese costume, especially her socks worn with thonged sandals, and the very wide belt of her kimono. She patiently explained the purpose of her attire and showed him hidden pockets in her sleeve.

We started our meal with the sashimi Manhattan. Served in a long, narrow lacquered box, skewers of sashimi are sculpted to represent the New York skyline, building-by-building, complete with two rivers of seaweed. Even kids who wouldn't think of eating raw fish love the spectacle of this dish. For those of us who do eat sashimi, Inagiku's version is superb. The texture and flavor are perfect; it is so delicate that it melts in the mouth. Our favorite entree is the steak Ishiyaki. First, a large sizzling stone is placed in front of you. Sirloin strips, so tender they can be cut with a chopstick, are cooked on the stone and eaten directly from it. To cook Shabu-shabu, a diner dips clear noodles, vegetables, and wafer-thin slices of steak into seasoned boiling water. Other notable items are the seafood or lobster tempura, both cooked in a very light batter and served in a wooden box.

Dinner here would not be complete without one of Inagiku's artful desserts. The bavaroise is a towering display of chocolate discs layered with white chocolate- and green tea-flavored creams. The ginger pear tart is served over vanilla ice cream and garnished with kiwi and blueberry. In response to Sam's request for plain ice cream with chocolate, the kitchen created a basket of sculpted white chocolate leaves cradling a scoop of vanilla ice cream. Sam was in heaven, and it made for a wonderful end to a very special dinner.

185

JACKSON HOLE

521 3rd Ave. (at 35th St.)

(679-3264

🚇 6 to 33rd St.

Hours:
10:30 AM - 1 AM

Brunch:
Sat & Sun: 10:30 AM - 3 PM

💳 AMEX only **$**   **Entertainment:** No

Note: Rest rooms can accomodate wheelchairs, but do not have railings.

Immensely popular with kids, the five locations of Jackson Hole are all pretty much the same, varying mostly in size. Decorated with old metal Coke signs, snowshoes, and black and white Old West photos, these restaurants can get a little rowdy, especially as the evening progresses. We generally choose a table in the rear of one of the dining rooms, which are furnished with butcher block tables under hanging Tiffany-style lamps.

The staff is very friendly to kids and courteous about cleaning up spills. There is a good children's menu with items such as burgers, chicken breast on a bun, chili, tuna sandwiches, and grilled cheese, for $3.50 to $5, including fries and a drink. The menu sheet is also a small activity page.

The regular menu is enormous, with around 200 listed items, including 39 types of beef or turkey burgers and an equal number of varieties of the house's special marinated chicken. With all the appetizers, salads, sandwiches, omelets, Mexican food, and blue plate specials, your biggest dilemma of the evening may be choosing what to eat. Sodas, shakes, milk, juice, beer, wine and coffee are available. We suggest you try the Jackson Hole brand root beer which is served with its own frosty mug. For dessert, try the waffles or ice creams, pies, and cakes.

Other locations:

Upper East Side: 232 E. 64th St.
(between 2nd & 3rd Aves.) 371-7187

Upper East Side: 1611 2nd Ave.
(between 83rd & 84th Sts.) 737-8788

Upper East Side: 1270 Madison Ave.
(at 91st St.) 427-2820

Upper West Side: 517 Columbus Ave.
(at 85th St.) 362-5177

JEKYLL & HYDE CLUB

1409 6th Ave. (between 57th & 58th Sts.)

℡ 541-9517 & 800-867-4933

🚇 B,Q,N,R to 57th St.

Hours:
Lunch & Dinner: 11 AM - 2 AM
Brunch: No

 $$ **Entertainment:** Yes

It may seem crazy to go to a restaurant with kids knowing that there will be at least a 45-minute wait, but the midtown Jekyll & Hyde Club is always worth it. While we wait, Sam and his friends like to talk about what's on the outside. The front of the building has been decorated to resemble an ancient temple, complete with tumbling columns and large stone masks and skulls. Look up and you'll see an old propeller-style airplane crashing into a pyramid on the roof. Four skeletons dance across the top ledge and others climb the facade (from their tattered clothing, we take them to be the remains of adventurers and explorers). Down at street level, the door is attended by doormen right out of *Indiana Jones*. Once inside, you will be met by a ghoulishly-dressed host who will lead you into a small room where the story of the Jekyll & Hyde Club is told. He also may ask you to loosen up by doing things like screaming.

Try to be seated in the first- or second-floor dining rooms. (The second floor balcony tables are our favorite.) Those locations afford the best views of the entertainment and skulduggery that will fill your evening. We don't recommend sitting in the third-floor ObservatOry, because it is glassed in, and somewhat removed from a lot of the goings-on.

We suggest that you stick with the lower-priced basics like burgers, pizzas, salads, and sandwiches (including the monster PB&J and grilled cheese). There is also BBQ or grilled chicken, steaks, shrimp tempura, fish, and pasta. The portions are so large it's not necessary to order both an entree and a starter. Kids can easily split orders and still have plenty to eat. Drinks include soda and juice, and the full bar specializes in 250 different types of beer (including three Trappist varieties). We recommend trying a specialty drink (non-alcoholic versions are available), even though they are expensive, because you get a choice of souvenir glasses, including skull mugs and miniature canteens.

The Jekyll and Hyde Club has taken the combination of dining and tongue-in-cheek ghostly entertainment to the limit. The portraits on the walls have roving eyes, and heads of alligators, rhinos, and giant swordfish either move and talk or have kicking feet sticking out of their mouths. There are scientific displays of insects and animals — some we may recognize, some seem to be the results of imaginary experiments gone awry. Television monitors play spooky black and white movies, and the sound system is a combo of kitschy rock and roll and horror movie soundtracks. You will be entertained by as diverse a group as mad scientists wandering in their lab coats (often with their slightly crazed wives following them), explorers in pith helmets, or even Dr. Jeykll himself reliving his transformation into Mr. Hyde. The many statues and props come to life from time to time, and if anyone in your party is celebrating anything at all (birthdays, graduations, anniversaries, etc.) be sure to tell a staff member — who knows, Zeus or the talking Sphinx may even decide to chat with you! The staff is attentive and very friendly, especially to families with children. There is a lot of security, so kids can roam fairly freely, studying all the bizarre appropriations. This all may be too scary for pre-schoolers, but if your family is up for a wonderfully camp evening of food and entertainment, Jekyll and Hyde is hard to beat.

JOHN'S PIZZERIA
260 W. 44th Street
(between Broadway & 8th Ave.)

(Not available at press time
🚆 1,9,2,3,7,N,R to Times Sq.;
A,C,E to 42nd St.

Hours:
11:30 AM - 11:30 PM
Brunch: No

NOT RATED

💲

Entertainment:
Watching the pizzas being made

Many kids and adults alike rate John's as the best pizza in New York City. Partly it's because the thin-crust pizza is really terrific, but it's also because the friendly helter-skelter activity makes everyone feel right at home. There are 54 varieties of pizza, as well as pastas and salads. Despite the famous "no slices" policy, these pies are so fabulous that customers keep coming back for more.

All four locations feature their trademark coal-fired brick ovens, and when kids go over to watch their pizzas being made, the chefs really ham it up. Expect a wait if you go at peak dining times, but even that will be worth it because of the staff's great attitude and the spectacular New York "fold-over"-style pizza (so-called because the best way to manage a slice is to fold it lengthwise). Beverages are beer, wine, and soda. There are no desserts.

Coming to Times Square in the spring of 1997 is what promises to be the largest and most spectacular John's Pizza yet. From the street, diners will walk through a bar area with a 20-foot-high skylight to a 400-seat dining room that features a five-story-high stained glass dome that was once part of a chapel. The decor will be similar to that of the Lincoln Center John's (see review), with a wraparound dining loft and a lot of natural wood. The four brick pizza ovens will be visible from all dining areas.

Other locations: (See reviews.)

Greenwich Village: 278 Bleecker St.
(between 6th & 7th Aves.) 243-1680

Upper East Side: 408 E. 64th St.
(between 1st & York Aves.) 935-2895

Upper West Side: 48 W. 65th St.
(between Central Park W. & Columbus Ave.)
721-7001

LUCKY'S BAR & GRILL
60 W. 57th St. (at 6th Ave.)

(582-4004

B,Q to 57th St.

Hours:
Sun-Thu: 7:30 AM - 12 midnight
Fri & Sat: 7:30 AM - 1 AM

Brunch:
Sat & Sun: 7:30 AM - 3:30 PM

$$ **Entertainment:** No

We stop into Lucky's for lunch when we're in the neighborhood and don't want to deal with the long lines at the nearby theme restaurants. The food is well prepared, the service friendly and efficient, but it is 57th Street, after all, so the prices tend to be a little high.

The restaurant has the feel of a classy casual brasserie, with a high ceiling, mirrored columns, milk-glass lamps, and walls decorated with interesting black and white photos of Manhattan. There is a classic dark wood bar and the tables in the bustling dining room are covered with checked tablecloths and surrounded by comfortable chairs or banquettes. It's hard even to hear the jukebox over the din of the diners, so kids can be a little loud.

The menu is the same all day except for the weekend brunch. Items kids might like include the thin-crusted pizzas ($9.95), pastas (half portions for $7.50), and grilled chicken ($13.95). Other choices include salads, a delicious yellowfin tuna tortilla, grilled fish, and steak. The beverages are milk, juice, sodas, and coffee; there is a full bar as well and an extensive wine list. Desserts include ice creams, brownies, tiramisu, and fruit.

MANHATTAN CHILI COMPANY
1500 Broadway (entrance on 43rd St.)

☎ 730-8666
🚇 1,2,3,N,R,S to Times Sq.;
   B,D,F to 42nd St.

Hours:
Sun & Mon: 11:30 AM - 11 PM
Tue-Sat: 11:30 AM - 12 PM

Brunch:
Sat & Sun: 11:30 AM - 3:30 PM

 $-$$ **Entertainment:**
                     Menu coloring, TV

We like the Manhattan Chili Co. so much we followed it uptown when it moved from the Village. The official $5.50 kids' menu features a dynamite black-and-white cartoon of a chili-ized Times Square for kids to color (crayons are provided), and food choices including chili with taco chips, or hot dogs or chicken fingers with fries. (The owner's ten-year-old daughter Alexandra suggests you try the chicken fingers served with honey). The regular menu offers burgers, fajitas, quesadillas, salads, nachos, dips and chips, and of course, many varieties of delicious chili. Our favorites are the flavorful Numero Uno — classic beef chili — and the mildly spicy Totally Vegetable. The High Plains Turkey chili is also very popular, and for those of you who like a really hot chili, try the jalapeno-loaded Texas Chain Gang.

193

Served with rice and a choice of two toppings, the chilis are $7.25 to $8.25. Desserts include gelato with chocolate sauce. Sodas, milk, and frozen fruit drinks (with and without alcohol) are served.

The food, however, is not the only reason the Manhattan Chili Company is one of our favorites. We love the fact that the restaurant itself is like one big cartoon. The walls are covered with fabulous 3-D cartoon art, including new views of New York City, and a row of high-steppin' Carmen Miranda chilies. And while most of the tables are covered with checked vinyl tablecloths, one table is shaped like a huge red chili. The restaurant is quite noisy, so kids can be a little loud. Plus, the TV at the smallish bar shows the Cartoon Network, a big point with Sam.

MARKET DINER

572 11th Ave. (at 43rd St.)

 695-0415

 A,C,E to 42nd St.

Hours:
Open 24 hours a day
Brunch: No

Entertainment: Menu coloring

While other restaurants may strive to imitate the diner theme, the Market Diner is the real thing. Walking in here is like stepping back in time — nothing much has changed since the diner was built in 1964. Check out the snakeskin vinyl booths, the white Formica tabletops with gold sparkles, the yellow Barbarella globe lights that hang over the sandwich counter, and the revolving pie display. The same songs play today as they did then, only now they're called oldies. And with its no-glam location near the Javits Center, Market Diner has the bonus of its own free parking.

The lengthy menu starts with eggs, pancakes and waffles, continuing with bagels, cereal, and fruit. The prices are a bargain. Burgers, for instance, start at $2.95 ($1.50 more for fries and slaw) and go up to $4.10 for a bacon cheeseburger. It seems that every type of sandwich ever made is available here, at prices that range from $1.95 to $6.95 for a triple-decker. There are Italian dishes such as eggplant parmigiana and lasagna and Greek souvlaki and moussaka. Although chicken, steak, pork chops, and seafood are on the menu, we suggest that you stick to the burgers and sandwiches.

KIDS EAT NEW YORK

The $4.95 kids' menu offers burgers, chicken, turkey, roast beef, spaghetti, and fried fish, all with sides, a small soda or milk, and ice cream. The usual wide range of diner pies and cakes is available; beverages include shakes and jug wines. The cappuccino and expresso listings on the menu are one of the few signs of the nineties. The friendly service is slow, but if you happen to find yourself in this far-flung neighborhood at mealtime, the Market Diner is a good choice for a casual bite.

MICKEY MANTLE'S
42 Central Park S. (between 5th & 6th Aves.)

(688-7777

N,R to Fifth Ave.;
B,Q to 57th St.

Hours:
Mon- Sat: 12 noon - 12 midnight
Sun: 12 noon - 11 PM
Brunch: Sunday: 12 noon - 3 PM

 $$

Entertainment:
Memorabilia, TV monitors

Opened in 1989 by the All-Star Yankee himself, Mickey Mantle's is a quality family restaurant. The main menu, served all day, features all of No. 7's favorites, including chicken-fried steaks, smoked baby back ribs, and chicken or beef chili. There are also blue corn nachos, grilled and roasted vegetables, club sandwiches, low-fat fish and pasta dishes, and salads. Portions are generous. The kids' menu offers burgers, chicken fingers, macaroni and cheese, spaghetti and meatballs, but oddly enough, no hot dogs. Soda, milk, and juice are available and dessert treats include root beer floats, ice cream, and hot fudge or brownie sundaes.

The restaurant has a wholesome, informal club feeling to it. The front room overlooks Central Park and features a large horseshoe-shaped bar. Roomy granite-topped tables are surrounded by comfortable wooden chairs; the handsome booths have cordovan leather seats. A glass wall separates the front from the slightly more formal back room. And in the warmer months there is fun sidewalk dining, with all the bustle of Central Park South to continuously amuse the family.

Inside there is also a great deal of entertainment, all with a sports theme. Video monitors are strategically located and show current and memorable past clips from basketball, football, tennis, and other sports, as well as baseball. Sam especially likes the comedy sports spots. Fabulous sports memorabilia, some signed, are displayed throughout the restaurant. Kids are welcome to roam about to check out this impressive collection. Many of the photos, paintings and sculptures are for sale, as is much of the equipment; the (high) prices are discreetly marked.

Mickey Mantle, who died in 1995, was considered the most popular player of his era, having hit 536 home runs. We highly recommend his restaurant, now also part of his legacy. It's a home run for children of all ages.

MOONROCK DINER

313 W. 57th St. (between 8th & 9th Aves.)

(397-3131

▢ A,B,C,D,1,9 to
57th St./Columbus Circle

<u>**Hours:**</u>
Mon-Thu: 6:30 AM - 1 AM
Fri: 6:30 AM - no closing
Sat: Open 24 hours
Sun: Open until 1 AM

Brunch:
Sat & Sun: 11 AM - 4 PM

▬ $ **Entertainment:** No

Moonrock offers something not so easily found on 57th Street — regular food at reasonable prices. Almost 24 hours a day, you can slide into a booth and order a burger ($3.95, $5.50 with fries) and a shake ($2.75) for less than the tip at some of the theme restaurants down the street. The same menu is served all day, starting with breakfast favorites such as eggs any way you like them, omelets, pancakes, Belgian waffles with fruit, and New York bagels with cream cheese and lox. Classic sandwiches include tuna, roast beef, grilled cheese; salads such as spinach with feta and sun-dried tomatoes are reliably good. Prices top out at $7.95 for a turkey triple-decker or a Caesar salad with grilled chicken.

Service is fast and friendly, with big smiles for the kids. Asked if they will ever add a kids' menu, they answer, "Why?" We agree — they already have all the basics a family could want.

MOTOWN CAFE

104 W. 57th St. (between 6th & 7th Aves.)

581-8030

N,R,B,Q to 57th St.

Hours:
Sun-Thu: 11:30 AM - 11 PM
Fri & Sat: 11:30 AM - 1 AM
Brunch: No

$$ **Entertainment:** Yes.
Tues is Karaoke / live mike night.

 20+

In 1959, Barry Gordy left his job with Ford Motors and founded the Motown Record Company with "$800 and a dream." In 1995 the Motown Cafe opened, and it does a good job of presenting that dream. The restaurant is filled with memorabilia, including many autographed photos, sparkling beaded evening gowns, and flashy tuxedos. Posters from Motown artists such as Mary Wells, Marvin Gaye, the Four Tops, and the Temptations vie for wall space with advertisements glamorizing the 1960s automobile culture.

Located on the site of the famous Horn and Hardart automat, some of the details have been preserved, including the self-serve wall (which now displays gold records) and the famous clock. The area that once announced "Today's Specials" now lists all the Motown hit singles by year. The color scheme is strictly '60s — turquoise, red (including the snakeskin patterned banquettes), and silver gray. If your toddler should

199

spill a drink here, no problem — the tables are covered with vinyl tablecloths.

On the balcony of the dining room, a statue of a young Michael Jackson peers over the edge to watch the short floor show, performed every 15 or 20 minutes by the "Motown Moments." (You may find one of them crooning to the kids at your table.) In between shows, Motown hits alternate with music videos shown on screens and monitors located throughout the restaurant. The DJs orchestrating this entertainment are located in the second floor Radio Motown booth that resembles an airplane control tower.

A large menu of American fare includes sloppy joes, burgers, hot dogs, BBQ, chicken, ribs, pork chops and meatloaf. There are also salads, pastas, and fish. Beverage options include shakes, sodas, lemonade, milk, coffees, and a full bar. The dessert choices range from sundaes and cakes to fruit cobblers and pecan pie. But the entertainment and theme park atmosphere are what draw people. Lots of people. Two-hour waits (longer on Saturday nights in the summer) are not uncommon.

Sam loves going to the Motown Cafe. He thinks it's cool and he likes wandering around looking at all the memorabilia, happily reporting back what he has found. They love families here, and we suggest that you give them a try — just don't go at a peak time.

OLLIE'S NOODLE SHOP & GRILLE

200B W. 44th St.
(between Broadway & 8th Ave.)

☎ 921-5988
🚇 1,2,3,7,9,N,R,S to
42nd St./Times Sq.

Hours:
Sun-Thu: 11:30 AM - 12 midnight
Fri & Sat: 11:30 AM - 1 AM
Sun: 11:30 AM - 11:30 PM

Brunch: No

Entertainment:: No

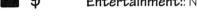

More than just a noodle shop, Ollie's offers tasty westernized versions of Cantonese, Mandarin, and Szechuan dishes. The extensive menu, with more than 200 items, has something for everyone, including plain grilled chicken and beef, and fish. One child we know won't try Chinese but loved Ollie's tuna kabob. (We make sure the sauces come "on the side.") The dumplings have a loyal following, as do the scallion pancakes and the lemon chicken. Prices are very reasonable, and the portions are large — order only one dish for each person and share. Beverages include sodas, beer and wine and there is a pot of Chinese tea on every table. The service is adequate, you don't have to ask for chopsticks, and fortune cookies appear right before you leave.

Other locations: (Both Upper West Side)
2315 Broadway
(at 84th St.) 362-3712
2957 Broadway
(at 116th St.) 932-3300

PLANET HOLLYWOOD
140 W. 57th St. (between 6th & 7th Aves.)

(333-7827

🚇 N,R,B,Q to 57th St.

Hours:
11 AM - 1 AM
Brunch: No

💳　$$　　　**Entertainment:** Yes

Owned in part by Bruce Willis, Sylvester Stallone, and Arnold Schwarzenegger, Planet Hollywood New York, the first one to open, has been entertaining diners since 1991. Filled with fascinating movie memorabilia, it is especially appealing to kids, who like to wander around the restaurant exclaiming at the many museum-quality displays of props and costumes from movies, including *Superman, Rocky, Star Wars, Terminator II* and *The Wizard of Oz.* All the items are shown with photos from the corresponding movies, and the displays are always changing.

It is wise to go early. There is always a line at peak hours, and it is worse in warmer weather. (Note: you cannot enter at all if your entire party is not present.) If you do have to wait, the kids can match their own hands with those of the stars on the handprint wall. Upon entering, you will be funneled into a bar area, where, with luck, you won't have to wait too much longer. When you are seated, the service is friendly and efficient.

The restaurant itself is decorated in a quasi-Hollywood style, with zebra-striped tablecloths and a carpet of planets, constellations, and shooting stars. Booths line the walls and tables fill the open areas of the irregularly-shaped rooms. Besides the memorabilia filling the walls and hanging from the ceiling, there are photos of movie stars everywhere. The staff wears either vests or Hawaiian-style shirts in the Planet Hollywood print. While you are eating, the videos of movie trailers and star interviews, as well as the general pandemonium, will keep most kids pretty well entertained.

Kids can choose from the usual fare of burgers or pizza, sodas and milk shakes, or can order grilled chicken, pork chops, fish, ribs, or strip steak. In addition, there are four kinds of pasta — vegetable or chicken penne, linguini with red sauce, and Thai shrimp linguini — beef, chicken, or shrimp fajitas; and chicken, steak or turkey club sandwiches. The portions are generous, and as there is no kids' menu, we recommend sharing. And if anyone is still hungry after all that food, there are some really good desserts, including Oreo mousse pie, brownie sundae, and apple strudel.

SKYLIGHT DINER

402 W. 34th St. (at 9th Ave.)

(244-0395

🚇 A,C,E,1,2,3,9 to 34th St.

Hours:

6 AM - 1 AM

Brunch: No

  $ **Entertainment:** No

We first noticed the Skylight Diner one evening, its striking cobalt blue, silver, and black decor dramatically lit up, looking like an Edward Hopper painting.

Even the cereal boxes look attractive in this setting, lined up next to the shiny brass Brugnetti espresso machine. A Brugnetti espresso machine in a diner at 34th and 9th Avenue? When a young hostess with the European accent shows you to your table, you'll begin to wonder if somehow you've been transported to SoHo. The front dining room has wonderful roomy booths and a wall of windows facing 34th Street. There is an attractive serpentine lunch counter with high-back stools, and a rear dining room with tables and chairs. Silver light fixtures that Sam says look like space ships hang over the tables. Tastefully framed posters of classic photographs of New York decorate the walls. (We especially like the one of construction workers taking their lunch break on a beam of an unfinished skyscraper, high over the city.)

The kids' menu is located on the back of the main menu, so don't overlook it — our waiter didn't even know it was there. It includes burgers, pasta, fish, or roast turkey with milk or soda and dessert, all for $4.95 to $5.95.

The extensive main menu offers soups, salads, sandwiches, burgers, omelets, pastas, pork and lamb chops, meatloaf, chicken, steak, and many varieties of fish. There are also daily specials. The food is good and basic, with a gourmet touch. Portions are generous, and despite the stylish details here, the prices are strictly diner. Beverage choices include juice, milk, shakes, soda, coffee and tea. As of this writing, they they are working on a liquor license. Until then, it's BYOB.

So if you happen to be at Macy's, Madison Square Garden, or at the Javits Center with your family, check out the Skylight.

STARDUST DINE-O-MAT

1491 Broadway (at W. 43rd St.)

(768-3170

N,R,S,1,2,3,7,9 to
Times Sq./42nd St.

<u>**Hours:**</u>
Sun & Mon: 7 AM - 11 PM
Tues-Thu: 7 AM - 12 midnight
Fri & Sat: 7 AM - 12:30 PM
Brunch: No

 $-$$ **Entertainment:** Sometimes
singing waiters after 9 PM

The Stardust Dine-O-Mat is the latest addition
to the Ellen Hart food empire, and it's a cause for
celebration for families who find themselves in the
Times Square area. Modeled after army canteens
of the forties, this two-story diner features
waiters outfitted in replicas of 1940s military
uniforms. There's lots of stainless steel, aluminum
and vintage advertising. Omelets on the menu are
named after bombers, burgers after big bands,
and there is a Victory Garden salad. Fancy versions of classic sandwiches include the Dagwood
(roast beef with grilled portobello mushrooms and
eggplant, roasted red peppers, and Romano
cheese with a balsamic dressing on a foot-long
roll), the G. I. Joe (grilled chicken on a roll with
fries), and the Bugle Boy (a triple-decker BLT).

All this translates into a lot of choices for kids
and adults, even without all the other standbys
on the menu. There are loads of shakes, malts,
sodas, coffees, teas, and milk plus beer and wine.
The ice cream and cake menu is impressive.

The light-hearted staff welcomes families and makes this a great stop for an inexpensive lunch or pre-theatre dinner.

TELEVISION CITY

74 W. 50th St. (at 6th Ave.)

(333-33TV (333-3388)

🚇 B,D,F to Rockefeller Center;
N,R to 49th St.;
1,9 to 50th St.

Hours:
6 AM - 2 AM
Brunch: No

▬ $$-$$$ **Entertainment:** Yes

Opened in the spring of 1997 by Regis Philbin, Susan Lucci, Joan Rivers, Michael Tucker, Jill Eikenberry and restaurateur David Liederman (of David's Cookies, Chez Louis, and Luna), Television City brings a new dimension to the genre of theme restaurants. The restaurant has been designed to feel like a real television studio, including a blue-screen room and an interview newscast set. Diners can participate in "Vote-A-Vision," an interactive game that can be played from their tables. They also may be "actors" in mock television news, weather, and talk shows, which will be broadcast over the 130 in-house screens, along with old TV clips, and promos for new shows. Sam advises all kids to plan out their "show", and for $20 you can purchase a video take-home copy of the program you participate in.

KIDS EAT NEW YORK

The menu reads like a TV guide with a smiley face icon indicating cool food for kids. Burgers (with fries and onion rings), penne with tomato sauce, cheesy fettucine, chicken fingers, and grilled cheese are available from $7.95 to $12.95. The crispy fried chicken in a lunchbox became the instant favorite for Sam and his friends because you can take it home. ($26 with the lunchbox; $13.95 without.) Also offered are salads, a selection of seafood including steamed mussels and delicious wasabi crusted salmon, grilled hanger steak, and the chef's specialty — roasted chicken. For dessert we recommend the creamy and tart key lime pie, pound cake with strawberries, and the super hot fudge sundae made with chocolate chip cookie ice cream.

VIRGIL'S REAL BARBEQUE

152 W. 44th St. (between 6th & 7th Aves.)

☏ 921-9494

🚇 1,2,3,N,R,S to Times Sq.;
B,D,F to 42nd St.

Hours:
Sun: 11:30 AM - 10 PM
Mon: 11:30 AM - 11 PM
Tue-Sat: 11:30 AM - 12 midnight
Brunch: No

$$ **Entertainment:** No

From the placemats at Virgil's comes this description of barbeque: "The premiere ethnic food of the South, a catalyst for great debate, a method of cooking, a cultural rite." And when the folks who brought us Carmine's, Ollie's, and Docks decided to open a BBQ joint in Manhattan, they ate their way across 14 southern states to create a menu that combines the best of all BBQ.

A blend of hickory, oak, and fruitwoods are used, and their perfume drifts lazily throughout this large restaurant. Each dish has its own distinct full-smoked flavor, even sides of collard greens and beets. The kitchen handles delicate items such as fish as deftly as it does the more traditional ribs, chicken, and steak. Our friend Rick, a life-long burger aficionado, tells us that Virgil's makes the tastiest ones he's ever had. The food is so good here that it's hard not to pig out.

The $4.95 kids' menu offers grilled cheese, chicken tenders, burgers, and flat dogs (franks split lengthwise), all served with fries. Soda selections include such southern favorites as birch beer, cream soda, and Orange Crush. Homemade lemonade, shakes, ice cream sodas, and milk are also available. Noisy kids won't be heard above the other diners, the country rock, and Delta blues.

The entrees, which average $15, come with a choice of two sides and a mini loaf of delicious corn bread. Portions are huge. The BBQ sandwiches, burgers, and po'boys will run you about half the cost of the entrees. Other options include specials such as Friday's Chesapeake clambake (lobster, shrimp, codfish, clams, mussels, corn on the cob, and potatoes) for $19.95. Folks rave about their desserts, especially the chess pies, and if you simply can't decide what to order, you can opt for the dessert sampler: pecan, peanut butter, chocolate chess, and key lime pies, plus banana pudding. The staff members are terrific, and have great senses of humor.

The owners have gone to great pains to create a sense of authenticity. (Though unlike roadside BBQs, the rest rooms are immaculate.) The space was completely gutted, down to the basement, and rebuilt in imitation of a real southern BBQ shack, starting with the tacky blinking neon sign out front. The downstairs dining room is pure 1950s diner, while the upstairs resembles a roadhouse with worn wood floors, wood-paneled walls crowded with framed pictures of cows, pigs, ranches and other BBQ restaurants, menus, aprons, and newspaper articles about cook-offs. From the second-floor balcony there is a great view of the vintage bar and its offerings of at least 100 bottles of beer on the wall.

EMPIRE STATE BUILDING
34th St. & 5th Ave.
• •

☎ 736-3100

🚇 6 to 33rd St.;
B,D,F,Q,N,R to 34th St.;
1,9,2,3 to 34th St.

OBSERVATORIES
To reach the observatories, take the specially
marked escalator and elevators.

Hours: 9:30 AM - 12 Midnight

Admission: Adults - $4.50; Seniors &
Kids 5 to 11 - $2.25; Kids under 5 - Free

Combo ticket with Skyride: Adults - $12.50;
Seniors & Kids - $8.25

Combo tickets with Skyride, a $3.50 savings, can
be purchased only at the observatory ticket
office.

*Not suitable for kids under five. Kids under three
and pregnant women are not allowed onto Skyride.*

Combo ticket with Transporter (1 ride):
Adults - $11.50; Seniors & Kids - $7.50

Tip: Save $1.25 - $1.50 with these combo tickets,
which can be purchased at the Transporter
counter, where the lines are much shorter than at
the Observatory ticket office.

*Kids under 48" and pregnant women are not allowed
on Transporter.*

Note: All ticket prices are subject to change.

They say that on a clear day you can see eighty
miles. That is, if you happen to be on the 102nd
floor of the Empire State Building. Even on a
not-so-clear day, the views of New York and

KIDS EAT NEW YORK

New Jersey are impressive from both the 86th- and 102nd-floor observatories. But be forewarned — you must go early, even on weekdays, as this is an extremely popular destination. Last year alone, 2.5 million people made the journey to the top. We suggest you arrive no later than 9 AM and preferably buy your tickets prior to your visit. (Even the ticket booths develop massive lines immediately upon opening.) We also recommend that you take the series of elevators directly to the 102nd-floor deck, as shortly after 10 AM the line will have become too long for any child's patience. The view from the 86th floor is also amazing and there is a lot more room to move around, so if you don't make it to the 102nd floor, don't worry.

Built in 1931 as the tallest structure in the world, the Empire State Building was constructed in only 19 months. The 102nd floor was originally designed (but never used) as a mooring dock for dirigibles. The top of the needle, at 1,454 feet, is the world's tallest television tower, providing broadcasting services to three TV stations and 14 FM radio stations. Its limestone and granite exterior trimmed with stainless steel is so strong that it even withstood a plane crashing into the 79th floor in 1945.

There is a gift shop and a snack bar on the 86th floor with the usual hot dogs, pretzels, popcorn and cookies. You can also get ice cream, sodas, juice, and coffee there.

SKYRIDE FLIGHT SIMULATOR
2nd Floor, Empire State Building

• •

☎ 279-9777

Hours: 10 AM - 10 PM daily

Not suitable for kids under five. Kids under three and pregnant women are not allowed onto this ride.

Admission:
Adults - $11.50; Children & Seniors - $9.50

Combo ticket with Observatory:
Adults - $12.50; Seniors & Kids - $8.25

Combo tickets, a $3.50 savings, can be purchased only at the observatory ticket office.

Tip: Buy the combo ticket for kids and seniors even if you plan only to go on the Skyride. It is $1.25 less than the individual Skyride ticket.

Note: Ticket prices are subject to change.

Narrated by *Star Trek's* Scottie, the Skyride is a 20 minute motion-simulated flight tour that zooms over, through, around, and under New York City before crashing into it.

Near the Skyride is a good gift shop, and a little snack bar selling fast food and beverages. There's no place to sit down and we suggest you plan to feed your family elsewhere. (See listings at the end of this entry.)

TRANSPORTER THRILL THEATER

Concourse (lower) Level, Empire State Building,
opposite Observation Deck ticket office.

• •

☎ 947-4299

Hours: 9 AM - 10 PM continuous showings

Note: Kids under 48" and pregnant women are not allowed on this ride. Seniors and recent hospital patients are asked to exercise their own judgement.

Admission:

Single Ride:
Adults - $8.50; Seniors & Kids - $6.50

Single Ride/Observatory combo ticket:
Adults - $11.50; Seniors & Kids - $7.50
(Tip: Save $1.25 - $1.50 with these combo tickets.)

Both Rides:
Adults - $14.50; Seniors & Kids - $10.50
(Tip: Save $2.50 with these combo tickets.)

Both Rides/Observatory combo ticket:
Adults - $16.50; Seniors & Kids - $10.50

Tip: Save $2.25 - $3.50 with these combo tickets; also, buy your tickets at the Transporter counter, as the lines are much shorter than at the Observatory ticket office.

Located on the lower level is the new computer-synchronized, motion simulation Transporter Theater, where you literally "hang onto your seats". As of this writing, the action movies now showing are "Dino Island" and "Secrets of the Lost Temple." Both seem longer than their actual five minute lengths, as you experience Jurassic Park- and Indiana Jones- type adventures through the use of visual, sound, and motion effects.

Not too far from the Empire State Building are the following restaurants that we suggest you consider (see reviews):

BRYANT PARK CAFE Bryant Park at 42nd St. (between 5th & 6th Aves.) 575-0733

PATSY'S PIZZERIA 509 3rd Ave. (at 34th St.) 689-7500

HUDSON PLACE 538-540 3rd Ave. (at 36th St.) 686-6660

JACKSON HOLE 521 3rd Ave. (at 35th St.) 679-3264

On the Mezzanine (street) level of the Empire State Building are three more restaurants:

BIG APPLE COFFEE SHOP/DINER

Mezzanine level, Empire State Building

(594-9570

Hours:

5:30 AM - 5:30 PM

Brunch: No

▬ $ **Entertainment:** No

This typical New York deli offers burgers, omelets, quiches, salads, and sandwiches. The kids' menu offers grilled cheese and hot dogs with fries. Milkshakes are served as well as milk, juice, lemonade, sodas, coffee, tea and ice cream desserts. The food is just OK, and we don't go out of our way to eat here, but it's a good solution if you have hungry kids who must eat now!

215

AU BON PAIN

Mezzanine level, Empire State Building

℅ 502-5478

Hours:
Mon-Fri: 6:30 AM - 9 PM
Sat: 8 AM - 8 PM
Sun: 8 AM - 4 PM
Brunch: No

 $ **Entertainment:** No

Like the rest of the Au Bon Pain croissant and coffee shops, this one offers pastries, croissant
sandwiches, soups, and salads. Beverages include
fresh OJ and other juices, milk, soda, coffee and
tea. The tasty food served in clean surroundings
makes this a good choice when a quick snack is
required.

HOULIHAN'S

Mezzanine level, Empire State Building

☎ 630-0339

Hours:
11:30 AM - 9:30 PM
Brunch: No

💳 **$$**   **Entertainment:** No

Part of a restaurant chain popular in the suburbs, Houlihan's is a bar/restaurant with sit-down service and a menu featuring nondescript appetizers, burgers, salads, and entrees like chicken and steak at inflated prices. The kids' menu includes spaghetti, chicken fingers, grilled cheese, and hot dogs. Milk, juice, and sodas are served.

MUSEUM OF MODERN ART

11 W. 53rd St. (between 5th & 6th Aves.)

● ●

☎ General Information: 708-9500
Exhibitions, Screenings, and Lecture
Information: 708-9480

TRANSPORTATION:

🚇 E,F to 5th Ave.;
B,D to Rockefeller Center;
N,R to 5th Ave.

Parking: Special rates to MoMA visitors with ticket validation (see Lobby Information Desk) at Square Industries, 17 E. 54th St.

Hours:

Sat-Tue: 11 AM - 6 PM;
Thu & Fri: 12 noon - 8:30 PM;
Closed Wed

Admission: $8.50 Adults; $5.50 Seniors & Students; Children under 16 and members free. Thu & Fri 5:30 - 8:30 PM: Pay as you wish. Special exhibitions average an additional $4 for non-members.

Of all the cultural attractions in New York, the Museum of Modern Art is one of the ones we visit the most, and yet we have only scratched the surface of what this great museum has to offer. Sam and his friends can relate to the artwork here, whether it's the drawing style of Picasso or the pop-art colors of Lichtenstein.

The sculpture garden features works by Matisse, Moore, Picasso, and Rodin in a beautiful setting. In the second-floor galleries you will find a magnificent collection of art of the first half of this century, presented in chronological order.

Starting with Post-Impressionists such as Cézanne, Seurat, and van Gogh, your kids should find a lot that is interesting as they wind their way through the sections representing Cubism, Dada, and Surrealism, including works by Kandinsky, Chagall, Mondrian, Picasso, Duchamp, Miró, Dalí, and Magritte. The third-floor galleries house the works of Lichtenstein, Warhol, Stella, and Johns.

Check newspaper listings for current special exhibitions. (Advance tickets, if necessary, can be purchased in the museum lobby or through Ticketmaster at 212-307-4545.) MoMA's film programs are screened daily, with tickets available at no additional cost on a first-come, first-served basis the day of the showing. You should also make it a point to inquire about MoMA's family programs. Led by the curatorial and education staff, they often include a hands-on art workshop for children with their adult companions.

Located near MoMA are the many family-friendly restaurants of 57th Street (see reviews in this chapter) as well as Television City, which is three blocks away.

For food at MoMA, there are three choices. In nice weather, try the snack kiosk in the sculpture garden. Dine casually at glass-topped cafe tables under the trees on the marble patio. The kiosk cart provides sandwiches, ice cream, beer, wine, sodas, and juice. We've seen families with bag lunches here, and it's a perfect place for strollers. In addition, there are two restaurants:

GARDEN CAFE

Ground level, Musuem of Modern Art

☏ 708-9500

Hours:
Sat-Tue: 11 AM to 5 PM
Thu-Fri: 12 noon to 7:45 PM
Wed: Closed
Brunch: No

▬ $$ **Entertainment:** Museum

The reasonably priced Garden Cafe is also located on the museum's ground floor, at the opposite end of the sculpture garden. A cafeteria-style operation, it offers many options for kids, such as burgers, pizza, and pastas, as well as fancier sandwiches and salads for the grown-ups. Fruit, desserts, milk, soda, juice, coffee, tea, beer and wine are available. Diners sit at industrial-looking silver plastic tables and chairs.

SETTE MOMA
BAR AND RISTORANTE

Second Floor, Museum of Modern Art

☏ 708-9710

Hours:
Lunch: 12 to 3 PM
(closed Wed)
Dinner: 5 to 10:30 PM
(closed Wed & Sun)
Brunch: No

 $$ **Entertainment:** Museum

Note: Free passes to the restaurant can be obtained through the Information Desk.
After 5 PM, enter at 12 W. 54th St.
Members receive a 20% discount for dinner only.

Located directly above the Garden Cafe, on the museum's second floor is the much fancier Sette MoMA Bar and Ristorante. Chic and contemporary, with a spare modern interior featuring ivory paper lights over the tables and sleek black chairs, the dining room has a long wall of windows overlooking the terrace and the garden below. Featuring elegant but overpriced Italian food, the service here is very good. Kids will nevertheless find this restaurant very stuffy, with little to offer them, and we suggest that you dine with them downstairs.

UPPER EAST SIDE & CENTRAL PARK

The **Upper East Side** is bordered by 59th Street to 96th Street and extends from the East River to Fifth Avenue.

For the purposes of this book we have included **Central Park**.

RESTAURANTS

ATTRACTIONS with RESTAURANTS
....

ANTICO CAFFEE

1477 Second Ave.(between 77th & 78th Sts.)

☏ 879-4824

🚇 6 to 77th St.

Hours:

Lunch:
Mon-Fri: 11:30 AM - 3:30 PM

Dinner:
Mon-Fri: 3:45 - 11:30 PM
Sat & Sun: 3:45 PM - 12:30 AM

Brunch:
Sat & Sun: 11 AM - 3:45 PM

$-$$ **Entertainment:** No

Note: Reservations weekdays only

Antico Caffee is a charming little Italian restaurant where everyone seems to be having a good time. Cheerfully decorated with geometric wall designs and light fixtures that are splashed with primary colors, this cafe is relaxed and friendly. The tables are paper-covered (bring your own crayons) and the banquettes, loaded with comfy cushions, can serve to station an infant seat. In season, the front of the restaurant turns into a bustling sidewalk cafe. The menu is divided into the traditional Italian categories, beginning with a selection of antipasti and salads. Entrees include grilled salmon, pan-seared red snapper, grilled or sautéed chicken, veal chops, and yellowfin tuna steaks. In addition, there are 23 pasta dishes, gourmet Italian sandwiches, and five types of delicious fold-over-style pizza. Portions are generous and well priced with the $6.85 lunch and brunch specials an excellent value. The friendly staff welcomes families, so don't be surprised if someone sits in on a game of UNO with your kids.

BARKING DOG LUNCHEONETTE

1678 3rd Ave. (at 94th St.)

☎ 831-1800

🚇 6 to 96th St.

Hours:

Breakfast only: 8 - 11 AM

Breakfast/Lunch: 11 AM - 4 PM

Lunch only: 4 - 5 PM

Dinner: 5 - 11:30 PM

Brunch: Sat & Sun: 8 AM - 4 PM

🚫 **$-$$**   **Entertainment:** No

Note: No reservations, however a big party can often be accommodated if you call 15 minutes ahead.

The Barking Dog is a comfortable, popular spot, a cross between a hip cafe and an upscale diner. It has the feel of a spanking clean 1950s sit-com kitchen, with lots of shiny silver and Formica and royal-blue accents. Cushioned booths or roomy wooden chairs surround the aluminum-edged tables that are located up a few steps from the sandwich counter. The tin ceiling and duct work are faux antique and the parchment-colored walls are decorated with vintage '40s and '50s advertisements, movie posters, and lots of pictures of dogs.

As there is usually a wait for dinner after 7:30 PM, try to arrive earlier. Kids love coming here, and there are always lots of them, even though there's no children's menu. Favorite meal choices of Sam and his friends include burgers, grilled cheese (not on the menu — ask for it), grilled chicken breast, lamb chops, and steak.

KIDS EAT NEW YORK

The kitchen will prepare plain pasta, but not in half portions. In addition to soda and milk (again, not on the menu — just ask), there are many fun choices from the soda fountain: shakes, malts, ice cream sodas, and egg creams. Sometimes there is live acoustic guitar music; crayons are always available, and be sure to ask to see the "Moe, the Dog" book.

The more mature diners will be interested in the nice range of salads, including Caesar, Cobb, and endive and watercress with apples, grilled potatoes, and Roquefort. Blue-plate specials change daily, as do menu entrees including sautéed Thai shrimp, Louisiana jambalaya, grilled leg of lamb, and vegetable and goat cheese lasagna. For dessert, try one of the Barking Dog sundaes or the delicious chocolate-raspberry truffle torte. And while there is no liquor license, it's OK to BYO.

BROTHER JIMMY'S

The combination of the laid-back atmosphere and FREE MEALS FOR KIDS makes both locations of Brother Jimmy's a magnet for families. That's right: two kids (under twelve) per adult can have anything on the Lil' Tykes menu — burgers, fried chicken, hot dogs, or macaroni — for free. And because these very casual college-style bar/restaurants feature a shack-like decor favoring plywood walls, corrugated tin ceilings, strings of colored lights, and wall ornaments like license plates and pig cartoons, rambunctious, happy kids are no problem.

BROTHER JIMMY'S BBQ

1461 1st. Ave. (at 76th St.)

☎ 288-0999
🚇 6 to 77th St.

Hours:
Sun & Mon: 5 - 11 PM
Tue-Thu: 5 PM - 12 midnight
Fri & Sat: 5 PM - 1 AM

Brunch:
Sat & Sun: 12 noon - 5 PM

 💳 $ **Entertainment:** Skee Ball

Expect hordes of kids in the early dinner hours at this self-proclaimed "pig heaven" whose motto is "Put some south in yo' mouth." While the cornbread may be a little dense and the pickles a little Vlassic, we love the tender meaty St. Louis ribs, the fried chicken, and the hickory smoke-flavored mashed potatoes. Plastic squirt bottles of finger lickin' good BBQ sauces and napkin dispensers for easy cleanup are on each table. Sunday is all-you-can-eat ribs and beer ($18.95) and Monday is lobsterfest night (your first lobster is $10.95; each additional lobster is $5.95). Sam likes the good-time rock music they play here as well as the Skee Ball machine. He also suggests that kids ask their parents to order the Swamp Water mixed drink. Delivered by a whistle-blowing waitress, it's served in a goldfish bowl with a toy alligator and lots of straws.

BROTHER JIMMY'S BAIT SHACK

1644 3rd. Ave. (at 92nd St.)

(426-2020

🚇 6 to 96th St.

Hours:
5 PM - 2 AM daily

Brunch:
Sat & Sun: 12 noon - 5 PM

▬ $

Entertainment:
Big screen TV, Ms. Pacman

The Cajun country cousin of Brother Jimmy's BBQ, the Bait Shack features shellfish, BBQ, and the largest TV screen on the East Side. The weekday dinner specials are a big draw. Monday's $9.95 baby back ribs are delicious. "Fat Tuesday" features jambalaya, gumbo, and crawfish at $6.50 a pound. Wednesday is an all-you-can-eat southern buffet for $7.95, and Thursday is an all-you-can-eat pasta night ($5). My favorite items are the bucket of peel-and-eat jumbo shrimp, market-priced around $10, and the raw oysters at a buck each (50¢ if you sit at the bar). The energetic good-time rockin' atmosphere offers lots for kids, including the many TVs and a Ms. Pacman. Oh, and Sam says, "Don't forget to check out the legs of the bar stools!" We'll let that be a surprise.

CALIFORNIA PIZZA KITCHEN

201 E. 60th St. (between 2nd & 3rd Aves.)

(755-7773

N,R,4,5,6 to 59th St.

Hours:
Sun-Thu: 11:30 AM - 10:30 PM
Fri & Sat: 11:30 AM - 11 PM
Brunch: No

 $

Entertainment:
Coloring books & crayons

Note: No reservations but call ahead if you're a large party and they'll try to hold a table.

California Pizza Kitchen loves kids, and Sam and his pals return the feeling. Set back from the street at the rear of a large public patio, the restaurant is very clean and cool with a California modern decor. Downstairs you can sit at a cafe table or at the oval black granite counter, where you can watch the pizzas being made in the wood-fired oven. We prefer to go up the wide circular staircase to one of the roomy booths. The generous spacing of the tables and the two-story wall of windows create a feeling of openness.

The simple kids' menu includes three types of four-slice pizzas (cheese, pepperoni, and BBQ chicken) and four kinds of pasta sauces (tomato, Bolognese, Alfredo, and butter) on either spaghetti, penne, or fusilli. These kids' meals run $4.50 to $5.50, including a soda or a glass of milk. For dessert, a kids' fudge sundae is $2.95.

The menu doubles as an activity sheet with a form you can send to the restaurant's Birthday Club.

California Pizza Kitchen encourages diners to try new things and guarantees that if you order something you don't like, they will replace it with something else. The main menu is extensive, with 27 varieties of pizza. Some of the inventive ones we've liked are the grilled chicken burrito pizza, which features poblano chilies, black beans, peppers, and onions topped with salsa and cheese; the Peking duck pie (duck meat, mushrooms, wontons, and hoisin sauce); and the strange Hawaiian pizza, which combines pineapples and bacon with a tomato sauce. We also suggest that you consider trying the spinach-artichoke dip appetizer, or one of the "CPK'sadillas," quesadillas made with slightly unusual fillings. The balance of the menu offers 16 types of pasta, along with appetizers, salads, and desserts, such as key lime pie, an upside-down cheesecake with a crust of vanilla wafers, and the tartufo, a ball of white chocolate ice cream coated with white chocolate chips. There is a full bar with microbrewed beers on tap.

While CPK is part of a national chain, you'd never know it by the atmosphere or attitude of the staff. The restaurant welcomes kids of all ages, including infants; there is even a baby-changing station in the rest room. A CPK cookbook is for sale, with the proceeds going to children's charities from coast to coast.

DALLAS BBQ

1265 3rd Ave. (between 72nd & 73rd Sts.)

 772-9393

 6 to 68th St. or 77th St.

Hours:
Sun-Thu: 11:30 AM - 12 midnight
Fri & Sat: 11:30 AM - 1 AM
Brunch: No

Entertainment: No

Among Sam's uptown pals, Dallas BBQ is high on the list. Specializing in large portions of smoky chicken, ribs, and burgers, we frequent the two uptown locations, one on the Upper East Side and one on the Upper West Side. Service is fast and friendly, and you will always see a lot of kids. The prices on the simple menu are quite low, with a BBQ half chicken costing $5.95 and ribs $8.95. Salads and burgers range from $4.95 to $7 and a basket of fried shrimp or chicken wings will only set you back $7.95. Be seated before 6:30 PM Monday through Friday, or before 5 PM on Saturday and Sunday, and you can order two half-chicken dinners for a total of $7.95. Oversized frozen cocktails are a specialty (kids can order theirs without alcohol), and in addition to the regular sodas and milk, there is a full bar.

The larger of the two uptown locations, this restaurant is set back from the street by a large brick patio which, in season, is a favorite for family dining and is protected from the weather by a large awning complete with ceiling fans. Even before you walk through the front door, you will be greeted by the wonderful aroma of the barbecue. The main dining room has an open feeling with cushioned blond wood chairs set around large, nicely-spaced tables. Mirrored columns, totem poles, Indian blankets, and longhorn cattle skulls decorate the restaurant, as well as a pretty white lattice ceiling.

Upper West Side location: 27 W. 72nd St. (between Columbus Ave. & Central Park West) 873-2004. (See review.)

Please note that we recommend only the two uptown locations of this chain. The two downtown branches on University Place and St. Mark's Place do not, we feel, represent the same dining experience.

E.A.T. CAFE

1064 Madison Ave. (between 80th & 81st Sts.)

(772-0022

🚇 6 to 77th St.

<u>**Hours:**</u>
Breakfast: 7 AM - 12 noon
Lunch: 12 noon - 6 PM
Dinner: 6 - 10 PM
Brunch: No

▬ **$$-$$$** Entertainment: No

The food and service at Eli Zabar's E.A.T. Cafe are superb and this is certainly *the* place to go for a casual lunch on the Upper East Side if your child enjoys gourmet food and price is not an issue. Both the quality of the food and the high prices here are legendary. To reach the cafe, with its black-and-white-checked marble floor, you must first walk through the deli, which gives you an amazing visual preview of the wide choice of freshly-made salads, such as haricots vert, marinated asparagus, whitefish, and calamari. In the cafe itself, the air is filled with the clatter of dishes and conversations. Each table has a basket of Eli's breads, which we quickly devour. Strollers are often present in abundance, as E.A.T. is very popular with mothers with young children.

Choosing something for picky eaters can be difficult here. We suggest you try the grilled free-range chicken, the roast beef sandwich, or the turkey club. The daily omelets and quiche are both excellent — light and full of flavor — and come served with a lovely salad of field greens.

The grilled cheese sandwich is probably the best I've ever tasted, but Sam won't consider it because it's made with "stinky" cheese (actually a French Gruyere). More sophisticated menu choices include cucumber and chevre on Eli's bread, ratatouille pizza, and a smoked salmon sandwich plate. At lunchtime expect to pay $8 for soups, $12 to $20 for sandwiches and entrees, and up to $45 for special dishes such as the Beluga caviar omelet. In addition to juice, there are fresh lemonade, sodas, coffee, tea, beer, and wine.

Another option is to come here for dessert. Kids will have a hard time choosing from the tempting display, which always includes a wonderfully rich chocolate cake; lemon, apple or raspberry tarts; cheesecake; brownies; and cookies. And to top off your E.A.T. visit, Sam suggests that you spend a few minutes next door at E.A.T Gifts — one of the best toy stores in the city, with many things well within the range of most kids' allowances.

EJ'S LUNCHEONETTE

1271 3rd Ave. (at 73rd St.)

📞 472-0600

🚇 6 to 77th St.

Hours:
Mon-Thu: 8 AM - 11 PM
Fri & Sat: 8 AM - 12 midnight
Sun: 8 AM - 10:30 PM
Breakfast/Brunch: Anytime

 $-$$ **Entertainment:** No

Note: Wheelchair access is difficult.

We liked the bright shiny atmosphere of EJ's as soon as we walked in. The booths, tin ceilings, 1940s advertisements, and old-fashioned ice cream counter all say family diner, and each of the three locations of this New York favorite is clearly kid-friendly. We are always greeted with a smile, and the cheerful staff never seems to have a problem with pint-sized diners who drop forks, spill milk, and generally make a little more noise than their parents would prefer. What is unexpected is how good the food is. The blue plate specials (served on blue plates) always feature several fish dinners, pastas, soups, and salads.

There is a special kids' menu that includes pancakes, French toast, eggs, burgers, tuna melts, PB&J, grilled cheese, and pasta, plain or with sauce. There are also a lot of dishes on the main menu that appeal to both kids and adults. Several youngsters that we know say this is their favorite restaurant.

As breakfast is served any time, half the menu is devoted to a wide variety of flapjacks, waffles, eggs, and omelets. For drinks, kids can choose from milk, juice, soda, and milk shakes. (Beer, wine, coffee and tea are also available for grown-ups.) And for the clean-plate club, there are rewards of cakes, brownies, pies, and ice cream.

Sam likes the fact that the waiters really do listen to his requests, especially the one for "no green stuff!" He also appreciates the quick service, that it's OK to be a little noisy, and that you don't have to be perfect at dinner, because, after all, EJ's is a diner.

Other locations:
West Side: 477 Amsterdam Ave.
(between 81st & 82nd Sts.) 873-3444
Greenwich Village: 432 6th Ave.
(between 9th and 10th Sts.) 473-5555

GOOGIES ITALIAN DINER
1491 2nd Ave. (at 78th St.)

(717-1122

🚆 6 to 77th St.

Hours:
Breakfast: 9 AM - 4 PM
Lunch & Dinner:
11 AM - 12 midnight
Brunch:
Sat & Sun: 9 AM - 4 PM

▬ $

Entertainment: TVs, crayons
& coloring books

Note: Wheelchair accessible but up a few steps. The staff will assist. Often a wait in peak hours and good weather — call ahead.

What happens when you mix Deco-inspired diner design with South Beach colors and a Cubist mural? Add burnished steel trim, a lot of mirrors, some marble, and you have Googies, a lively combination of diner motifs. The service is not only kid-friendly, but also baby-friendly, with waiters always ready to supply additional napkins or spoons or to clean up a toddler's spills. We prefer to sit in one of the larger turquoise leatherette booths, or in the warmer months, at one of the 16 tables in the front section, which opens into the sidewalk cafe. There are also many smaller tables and a long soda fountain counter (bar), that features multiple video monitors.

In the last year Googies has added crayons, coloring books, and the "Little Googies" menu. For $4.95, kids can choose from burgers, grilled cheese with or without ham, and chicken on skewers (all served with shoestring fries), or pasta with butter or red sauce. The rest of the family will have no problem selecting from the large Italian diner menu. In addition to a wide range of sandwiches and burgers, Googies offers pastas, salads, chicken, steak and meatloaf. If Sam and his friends aren't tempted by one of Googies' thick milkshakes, other drink options include milk, juice, soda, and a full bar for adults. For your dessert order, soda fountain sundaes compete with Italian cheesecake, tiramisu, and crème brûlée.

IL VAGABONDO

351 E. 62nd St. (between 1st & 2nd Aves.)

(832-9221

🚇 4,5,6,N,R to 59th St.;
B,Q to 63rd St.

<u>**Hours**</u>:
Lunch: Mon-Fri: 12 noon - 3 PM
Dinner:
Mon-Sat: 5:30 PM - 12 midnight
Sun: 5:30 - 11 PM
Brunch: No

▬ **$$**   **Entertainment:** Bocce court

10+

Note: No kids' menu but will do half orders. Wheel-
chair accessibility difficult

The special draw of Il Vagabondo is the bocce
court. That's right, an indoor bocce court, the only
one in the city and the only one I have ever heard
of in a restaurant. (Bocce is an Italian bowling
game, usually associated with parks or beaches.)
Diners are encouraged to take a break from their
meals to play a few games (there is no charge),
although, for insurance reasons, children are not
usually allowed on the court. They are able,
however, to watch the games and occasionally
older children have been allowed to play with
special permission from the manager and with
parental supervision.

Il Vagabondo occupies a space created from two
townhouses. Little expense went into the decor,
which consists mainly of black and white photos
of sports celebrities playing bocce and tables cov-
ered with red and white checkered tablecloths.

The restaurant features classic southern Italian family cooking; in fact, as you walk by the open kitchen, you can't help but notice that the chefs are speaking only Italian. We like the large open dining room off the kitchen, which has a view of the small back garden. Kids are welcome, and there are usually quite a few roaming the restaurant. The tables are a little close, which can be a problem for younger children, but as the dining crowd grows, so does the noise level, so kids talking a little too loudly are no problem.

Offering traditional Italian cuisine, the menu is divided into categories of appetizers, salads, pastas, and entrees. The classic entrees include veal, chicken, fish, and steak dishes that can be prepared "plain" for kids. The specials are worth considering, including the veal chop, the stuffed veal, and the seafood pastas, as well as the swordfish. Servings are large and kids should share orders, especially meat and fish entrees, which are served with a large side dish of pasta or a salad. Service, while very nice, can be a little slow, so make the most of your waiter when you see him.

JACKSON HOLE

232 E. 64th St. (between 2nd & 3rd Aves.)

☎ 371-7187

🚇 6 to 68th St.;
4,5,N,R to 59th St.;
B,Q to 63rd St.

Hours:
Mon-Sat: 10:30 AM - 1 AM
Sun: 10: 30 AM - 12 midnight
Brunch:
Sat & Sun: 10:30 AM - 3 PM

💳 AMEX only $ **Entertainment:** No

      6+

JACKSON HOLE

1611 2nd Ave. (between 83rd & 84th Sts.)

☎ 737-8788

🚇 4,5,6 to 86th St.

Hours:
Mon-Thu: 10:30 AM - 1 AM
Fri & Sat: 10:30 AM - 3 AM
Sun: 10:30 AM - 12 midnight
Brunch:
Sat & Sun: 10:30 AM - 3 PM

💳 AMEX only $ **Entertainment:** No

       6+

JACKSON HOLE

1270 Madison Ave. (at 91st St.)

📞 427-2820

🚇 6 to 96th St.

Hours:
Mon-Sat: 6 AM - 11 PM
Sun: 6 AM - 10 PM

Brunch:
Sat & Sun: 10:30 AM - 3 PM

💳 AMEX only   **$**   **Entertainment:** No

Note: At all three Upper East Side locations, rest rooms can accommodate wheelchairs but do not have railings

Immensely popular with kids, the five locations of Jackson Hole are all pretty much the same, varying mostly in size. Our favorites are 64th Street on the East Side and Columbus Avenue on the West Side. Decorated with old metal Coke signs, snowshoes, and black and white Old West photos, these restaurants can get a little rowdy, especially as the evening progresses. We generally choose a table in the rear of one of the dining rooms, which are furnished with butcher block tables under hanging Tiffany-style lamps.

The staff is very friendly to kids and courteous about cleaning up spills. There is a good children's menu with items such as burgers, chicken breast on a bun, chili, tuna sandwiches, and grilled cheese, for $3.50 to $5, including fries and a drink. The menu sheet is also a small activity page. The regular menu is enormous, with around 200 listed

243

items, including 39 types of beef or turkey burgers and an equal number of varieties of the house's special marinated chicken. With all the appetizers, salads, sandwiches, omelets, Mexican food, and blue plate specials, your biggest dilemma of the evening may be choosing what to eat. Sodas, shakes, milk, juice, beer, wine and coffee are available. We suggest you try the Jackson Hole brand root beer which is served with its own frosty mug. For dessert, try the waffles or ice creams, pies, and cakes.

Other locations:

Midtown: 521 3rd Ave.
(at 35th St.) 679-3264
Upper West Side: 517 Columbus Ave.
(at 85th St.) 362-5177

JOHN'S PIZZERIA

408 E. 64th St. (between 1st & York Aves.)

☎ 935-2895

🚇 6 to 68th St.

Hours:
Sun-Thu: 11:30 AM - 11:30 PM
Fri & Sat: 11:30 AM - 12:30 AM
Brunch: No

 $

Entertainment:
Watching the pizzas being made

Many kids and adults alike rate John's as the best pizza in New York City. Partly it's because the thin-crust pizza is really terrific, but it's also because the friendly helter-skelter activity makes everyone feel right at home. There are 54 varieties of pizza, as well as pastas and salads. Despite the famous "no slices" policy, these pies are so fabulous that customers keep coming back for more.

All four locations feature their trademark coal-fired brick ovens, and when kids go over to watch their pizzas being made, the chefs really ham it up. Expect a wait if you go at peak dining times, but even that will be worth it because of the staff's great attitude and the spectacular New York "fold-over"-style pizza (so-called because the best way to manage a slice is to fold it lengthwise). Beverages are beer, wine, and soda. There are no desserts.

The Upper East Side branch is reminiscent of a small, inviting Italian trattoria, with its simple

---

decor and festive printed tablecloths. Note: Half orders of pasta can be ordered for kids.

Other locations: (See reviews.)
Greenwich Village: 278 Bleecker St. (between 6th & 7th Aves.) 243-1680
Midtown: 260 W. 44th St. (between Broadway & 8th Ave.)
Note: Telephone number not available as of press time.
Upper West Side: 48 W. 65th St. (between Central Park W. & Columbus Ave.) 721-7001

MARY ANN'S
1503 2nd Ave. (at 78th St.)

📞 249-6165
🚇 6 to 77th St.

Hours:
Lunch: Mon-Fri: 12 noon - 4 PM
Dinner:
Mon-Thu: 5 - 10:30 PM
Fri & Sat: 4 - 11 PM
Sun: 4 - 10:20 PM
Brunch:
Sat & Sun: 12 noon - 4 PM

💳 No AMEX **$-$$**

Entertainment: Fri & Sat: Mariachi bands starting at 8 PM

8+

Mary Ann's, with four locations in Manhattan, is an ideal choice for good traditional Mexican fare at modest prices. With its "La Bamba" music, handmade tiles and stucco walls, punched tin star-shaped lamps, and Mexican blankets, you almost feel like you're in Tijuana. Be sure to go early — by 8:15 PM, every table will be filled and there will be a crowd at the bar waiting to eat.

First thing, Sam dives into the bottomless bowl of free chips and salsa. The homemade guacamole starter is served in a stone cornmeal grinder. The $3.95 kids' menu provides large servings of tacos, enchiladas, cheese quesadillas, chicken fajitas, or crispy flauta chicken rolls, all with rice, beans, or French fries. All the other dishes are ample too — we never leave hungry.

The sizzling fajitas, available in steak, chicken or vegetarian variations, served with a lot of fanfare, are probably the most popular dish on the menu, but you really can't go wrong with any of the classic Mexican combination plates. We have especially enjoyed the Santa Fe sirloin burritos, the taco and enchilada specials, and the Mary Ann's combo, a shrimp burrito and chicken tostado. Vegetarian varieties are also available. For something a little different, try the camarones Veracruz, a delicious preparation of sautéed jumbo shrimp. Like most of the other dishes, these are served with generous sides of rice, beans, and salad.

Our favorite Mary Ann's, this location is a little larger than the others and features mariachi musicians on the weekends. Dressed in traditional Mexican garb, they stroll from table to table, and for just a few dollars' tip they will serenade your little ones.

Other locations:
Chelsea: 116 8th Ave.
(at 16th St.) 633-0877
East Village: 80 2nd Ave.
(at 5th St.) 475-5939
Upper West Side: 2452 Broadway
(at 91st St.) 877-0132

PATSY'S PIZZERIA

1312 2nd Ave. (at 69th St.)

☎ 639-1000

🚇 6 to 68th Street,
    B,Q to 63rd St.

Hours:
Sun-Thu: 12 noon - 11 PM
Fri & Sat: 12 noon - 12 midnight
Brunch: No

🚫💳 $-$$ **Entertainment:** No

In the first quarter of this century, several young
Italian pizza chefs, including John of John's
Pizzeria, Tottono of Coney Island, and Patsy
Lancieri, learned their craft at Gennaro Lombardi's
restaurant. These chefs then went on to open
their own, now famous, pizzerias. The one Patsy
Lancieri opened in 1933 in East Harlem is still in
business, serving not only pizza but also salads,
soups, pastas, and desserts. His nephew, Patsy
Grimaldi, subsequently went on to open Patsy
Grimaldi's. Recently, four branches of Patsy's
Pizzeria have opened in Manhattan, all of which we
recommend for families

Patsy's Pizzeria offers brick-oven pizzas and an
extensive menu that includes appetizers, salads,
and pasta. The pizza ovens are in the dining rooms,
where you can watch the chefs at work. Pizzas
cost $10.95 and $12.95 and toppings are an additional $2 each. The small pizza is certainly big
enough for two kids. Salads and pastas are available in individual and family-sized portions.

Roughly twice the price of the generous single servings, the "big bowl" family orders are an excellent buy, easily serving a family of four.

The Upper East Side Patsy's is the newest location and is similar to the University Place branch in its warm Old Country design. Sitting at any of the simple marble tables, you can't miss the appetizing aromas of pizza baking in the brick oven. The menu also offers the restaurant's trademark individual or family-sized salads and pastas. Try to leave room for a cannoli or a piece of the delicious chocolate crunch cheesecake.

Other locations: (See reviews.)
Murray Hill: 509 3rd Ave.
(at 34th St.) 689-7500
Greenwich Village: 67 University Pl.
(between 10th & 11th Sts.) 533-3500
Upper West Side: 64 W. 74th St.
(at Columbus Ave.) 579-3000

PEPPERMINT PARK
1225 1st Ave. (at 66th St.)

(288-5054

🚇 6 to 68th St.

Hours:

Breakfast: Mon-Fri: 9 - 11 AM

Regular Menu:

Mon-Fri: 9 AM- 12 midnight

Sat & Sun: 9 AM - 2 AM

Brunch:

Sat & Sun: 11 AM - 4 PM

▭ $

Entertainment: No

As Peppermint Park is an ice cream parlor, it is designed for kids. It does, however, dish up a lot more than cones, sundaes, and banana splits. The menu offers hot dogs, burgers, chicken nuggets, and sandwiches — regular, triple-deckers, and grilled cheese. There are salads (Caesar, Nicoise, and chef), quiches, meal-sized crèpes, onion rings, and French fries. Alcoholic beverages are not served but they do offer milk, soda, lemonade, shakes, coffee and tea. For dessert you can enjoy sweet crèpes, Belgian waffles, strudel, cannolis, and eclairs, brownies, cookies, hazelnut torte, cheesecake, and carrot cake. They serve breakfast daily until 11 AM and brunch on the weekends. And if your kids finish all their food, you may decide to treat them to some penny candy on your way out.

The front take-out area has tempting displays of desserts and ice cream. The actual dining area is small — two little rooms with pretty floral upholstered seats, pine green walls, and Art

Nouveau lamps. The place is always filled with kids of all ages. On school holidays and weekends, you should phone ahead, especially since one birthday party can take over the entire table-service portion of the restaurant.

SARABETH'S

1295 Madison Ave. (between 92nd & 93rd Sts.)

☎ 410-7335

🚇 6 to 96th St.

Hours:
Breakfast:
Mon-Fri: 8 AM - 3:30 PM
Lunch:
Mon-Fri: 11:30 AM - 3:30 PM
Tea: 4 - 6 PM
Dinner:
Mon-Sat: 6 - 10:30 PM
Sun: 6 - 9:30 PM
Brunch: Sat & Sun: 9 AM - 4 PM

▭ $$-$$$ **Entertainment:** No

Note: Reservations for dinner only. Rest rooms for the handicapped are available in the adjacent Hotel Wales

Both of the Sarabeth's started out as bakeries — first on the West Side and later on the East Side. Later still, the Sarabeth's Cafe at the Whitney Museum was opened (see review).

Despite the high menu prices (appetizers average $7, dinner entrees $17), the restaurants continue to be popular because the food is skillfully prepared with quality ingredients. Sarabeth's serves a lot of children even though there is no kids' menu, probably because the comfortable ambiance suits diners of all ages. In fact, the West Side location has a sign for stroller parking, and at the East Side location there is a seating area next to the bakery counter, perfect for dining with a child asleep in a stroller. Unfortunately, neither restaurant takes brunch reservations, so you may have to wait for a table. For dinner, we strongly recommend that you make reservations.

The amiable staff does a good job of remembering regulars. The menu changes daily and is slightly different for each location. The smooth, buttery tomato soup and the crab cakes with baby greens are two of the appetizers that I most enjoy. We recommend the chicken pot pie with crispy cooked vegetables in a light pastry crust, the roasted red pepper and mozzarella ravioli in a fresh tomato sauce, and the grilled lamb with roasted potatoes. Even though we clean our plates, we always sample Sarabeth's incredible desserts (fruit tarts, chocolate cakes, melt-in-your-mouth brownies). But if you can't even contemplate the thought of another bite, you can purchase these baked goods to take home.

Other location:
Upper West Side: 423 Amsterdam Ave.
(between 80th & 81st Sts.) 496-6280

SERENDIPITY 3

225 E. 60th St. (between 2nd & 3rd Aves.)

(838-3531

N,R,4,5,6 to 59th St.

Hours:
Sun-Thu: 11:30 AM - 12 midnight
Fri: 11: 30 AM - 1 AM
Sat: 11:30 AM - 2 AM
Brunch: No

$-$$ **Entertainment:** Yes — toys can be purchased at the general store

Serendipity 3 is one of those great little restaurants that have been around forever (since 1954 in this case) and have only gotten better. The name comes from a fable about three princes the original owners fancifully identified with. This Art Nouveau ice cream parlor, with its eclectic general store filled with unusual toys, cards, and artsy glassware, is a delightful place to bring kids. The downstairs dining room has marble cafe tables with white metal chairs, ornate Tiffany lamps, and a mishmash of mirrors, Art Nouveau posters, and stained glass windows below its greenhouse ceiling. Up the spiral staircase are two parlor-style dining rooms that bespeak a faded bohemian French elegance.

Although desserts are what Serendipity is known for, we suggest that you consider coming for a complete meal. The menu is extensive — a full range of soups, salads, pastas, foot-long hot dogs, burgers and sandwiches, as well as crèpes (seafood, chicken, or chili), lemon chicken, and shrimp and vegetable brochettes. Look for the reasonably-priced specials. We usually stick to lighter fare so that we still have room for one of the delectable ice cream desserts. Sam likes the frozen hot chocolate, made from fourteen types of chocolate, frozen, then ground into slush. There are other frozen drinks, sodas, juices, milk, coffee, and tea. No alcohol is served.

And Sam feels the bathrooms are worth mentioning, too — they feature old-fashioned wooden tanks, the kind with a pull cord.

SOFIA

1022 Madison Ave. (at 79th St.)

(734-2676

🚊 6 to 77th St.

Hours:
Mon-Fri: 12 noon - 12 midnight
Sat-Sun: 12 noon - 1 AM
Brunch: No

▬ **\$\$-\$\$\$** **Entertainment:** Paper-covered tables (bring your own crayons)

Where to go for lunch or early dinner to be "seen" with children? Try Sofia, a loud and trendy restaurant that feels like a cross between St. Tropez and SoHo. One flight up a curving staircase with sunny frescos, the small dining room is packed with beautiful people, their beautiful kids, and a buzz of excitement. In warmer weather, the third floor balcony with its 20-foot tented ceiling and cobblestone floor is especially popular at lunchtime.

The signature dish is pizza (15 varieties), from classics to house specials, including mozzarella/prosciutto/tomato and smoked salmon/brie/dill. The crispy crust is incomparable, and it ought to be — it's baked in a moisture-free oven that uses lava rocks from Mt. Vesuvio, sand from Sardinia, and Sicilian sea salt. The appetizers, while expensive ($8.50 to $14), are delectable and artistically presented on oversized plates. For the adults, we suggest the tuna carpaccio, served with arugula and julienned carrots, zucchini, and scallions, or the baked artichoke hearts with scoops of buffalo mozzarella; both make a light lunch on their own. The penne with spicy sausage in a cream sauce is our favorite among the many pastas, which the kitchen will prepare plain on request. In addition, there are grilled chicken, beef, and fish dishes.

Sofia becomes crowded around 7 to 7:30 PM (and the staff becomes a little stretched). There is officially a no-reservations policy, but if you call in advance, and mention that you are bringing kids, they will do their best to hold a table.

TWINS

1712 2nd Ave. (between 88th & 89th Sts.)

987-1111

4,5,6 to 86th St.

Hours:

Dinner: 4:30 - 10:30 PM

Brunch: Sun: 11 AM - 2 PM

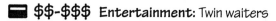
$$-$$$ **Entertainment:** Twin waiters

Note: KIDS EAT FREE Monday nights

The proprietors of Twins give a whole new spin to the idea of family business. Twins by birth, restaurateurs by avocation, they came up with a theme restaurant that employs hostesses, waiters, waitresses, busboys who have one shared qualification: they're all twins. Think you're seeing double? You are. We have been told that 27 pairs of twins are actually employed here. On any given night, many of the diners are twins, too, and they receive special attention (and seating preference) at this popular, hip restaurant.

The restaurant has a bar in the front and a medium sized dining room in the back. The eclectic decor works, as does the inventive and tasty menu. Appetizers range from "double" cheese fondue to gazpacho. There are salads, pizzas, and pastas plus steak, roasted chicken, and grilled salmon. The "twin" lobster special is very popular (and sells out); and we also recommend the pesto-stuffed tuna steak and the chili-seared beef tenderloin.

VINEGAR FACTORY RESTAURANT

431 East 91st St. (between 1st & York Aves.)

☎ 987-0885

🚇 6 to 96th St.

<u>Hours:</u>
(Open Sat & Sun only)
Breakfast: 8 AM - 12 noon
Brunch: 8 AM - 4:30 PM

💳 **$$**   **Entertainment:** No

A major brunch destination for East Siders, the Vinegar Factory offers the reknowned Zabar's-quality food at prices less than those at E.A.T. Set in an airy industrial loft overlooking the food market part of the complex, the restaurant's sunny decor combines wooden floors and whitewashed bricks with exposed steel joists, metal ductwork and large factory lamps. The pretty greenhouse in the back houses a second dining room. Classical music drifts in the background and the restaurant is filled with the buzz of conversations. Often the green Vinegar Factory balloons are on hand for the kids.

Open only for weekend brunch, expect to wait for a table if you arrive between noon and 2:30 PM. It will all seem worth it when you dive into the basket of Eli's delicious breads that awaits on each table. Everything on the menu is guaranteed to please: the omelets, the pizzas, the hefty sandwiches, and the cheese blintzes with home-made jam. The all-you-can-eat salad barrel is a big draw, especially at $12 for adults, and $6 for kids.

Regular breakfast items such as pancakes and eggs are served from 8 AM until noon. Beverages include milk, juice, coffee, and wine; we especially recommend the hot chocolate and the fruit smoothies. And if you still have room, those great Zabar's desserts are also served, including fruit tarts and carrot, chocolate, or cheese cake.

YURA & CO.

1645 3rd Ave. (at 92nd St.)

(860-8060

6 to 96th St.

<u>Hours:</u>
Breakfast Mon-Fri: 7 AM - 4 PM
Lunch: 11 AM - 4 PM
Early bird fixed price dinner:
Mon-Fri: 4:30 - 6:30 PM
Dinner: 6 - 9:30 PM

Brunch:
Sat: 7 AM - 4 PM
Sun: 8 AM - 4 PM

No AMEX **$$ Entertainment:** No

Note: Reservations not accepted for brunch

Looking for a simple yet beautiful place on the Upper East Side for either a relaxing lunch or a quick bite? We'd like to suggest Yura and Co. One side of it is a take-out shop filled with tempting breads, meats, salads and desserts that can be eaten at little cafe tables. The barn-board walls of this area are decorated with garlands and wreaths of dried bay leaves, and the white high ceiling forms a pleasing contrast.

To the right is the main cafe, more like a beautiful country house than a restaurant. Its tall windows are filled with a theatrical display of silk dogwoods, complete with songbirds and a moss floor; fica trees and Boston ferns surround a piano in the corner. Tablecloths printed with botanical illustrations cover the cafe tables and a beautiful Victoria espresso machine stands on the sideboard.

The back half of the space is occupied by the large kitchens required by this combined take-out, cafe and catering business. The chef's expertise is reflected in the lovely presentation of the wonderful-tasting food. Breakfast is available all day and includes muffins, scones, fruit plates and waffles. A $3.95 omelet is available weekdays until 11 AM. Kids might like the grilled cheese, roast beef, and tuna fish sandwiches and the tempting desserts. The small menu, which changes daily, offers salads, cold poached salmon, roast leg of lamb, and soft-shell crabs. Beverages include milk, juices, sodas, teas and coffees. No alcohol, but you may BYO. The cafe, which can seat about 60, is also open for dinner, but we suggest coming with kids only for breakfast or lunch. The service is very good, and babies are welcome.

CENTRAL PARK

. . . .

On weekends there are pushcart vendors throughout the park who sell hot dogs, pretzels, ice creams, and sodas.

In addition, there are two places that have indoor food service that we recommend:

BOATHOUSE CAFE

In Central Park
East Drive (at 74th Street)

(517-2233
🚇 A,C,B, to 72nd St./CPW;
6 to 77th St.

Hours:
Lunch Mon-Fri: 12 noon - 4 PM
Dinner: 5:30 - 10 PM
Brunch:
Sat & Sun: 11 AM- 4 PM

💳 $$$ **Entertainment:** The view

Note: Park trolley transportation: 7 PM - Closing Instead of highchairs or booster seats, plastic chairs are stacked.

A highlight of any family outing to Central Park is a meal at the Boathouse Cafe. The setting can't be beat for beautiful scenery — rowboats on the lake, a stunning sunset, or twinkling skyscrapers after dusk. The boathouse can be reached from the 72nd Street entrance to the park either by foot or by taking the trolley that runs every 15 minutes from 7 PM until the last diner leaves.

During the week there isn't usually a wait (you'll feel like you own the place), but on weekends you may spend a short time in the comfortable bar area, a yellow and white striped tent, until a table frees up.

The cafe consists of the boathouse and a multilevel patio area sheltered by a large white heated tent. There are flowering plants everywhere; these, and many other small details, make this place feel special. The boathouse is enclosed by large windows and has a wonderful elegance that includes Oriental rugs on the slate floor, a grand piano, and a white cockatoo. It all has the feel of a luxurious country club, and indeed, the staff treats every-one, including infants, as if they were VIPs.

The kid's menu (you have to ask for it) offers chicken tenders, burgers, hot dogs (all with fries), and pasta for $7.50. The main menus differ little from lunch to dinner and are a nice blend of American and Italian, with appetizers, soups and salads, gourmet sandwiches, pastas, and entrees such as grilled fish, roasted chicken, and steak. Prices are a little steep, and the service can be a little slow (the kitchen is a long way off), but the bucolic ambiance can't be beat.

Sharing the kitchen is the Boathouse Express, open daily from 9 AM until 5 PM. (Breakfast is available until 11 AM.) This take-out counter offers hot dogs, burgers, fries, chili, deli sandwiches, and salads such as chicken, tuna, and fruit, as well as beverages. There are picnic tables inside the boathouse and some outside cafe tables, though they don't face the lake. Many families prefer to bring blankets and picnic on the grass.

KIDS EAT NEW YORK

Boxed lunches are available for $8.50. There is also a small ice cream shop that offers cones, sundaes, banana splits, and root beer floats.

WOLLMAN RINK CAFE

In Central Park
Between the East and Center Drives (at 63rd St.)

(396-1010

N,R, to 59th St./5th Ave.
4,6, to 59th St.
B,Q, to 57th St./CPS

Hours:
Mon: 10 AM- 5 PM
Sun,Tues-Thurs:
10 AM- 9:30 PM
Fri & Sat: 10 AM - 11 PM

Brunch: No

$

Entertainment:
Skating rink, miniature golf

Located at the Wollman Memorial Skating Rink, this cafe is really a snack bar serving the usual assortment of hot dogs, pizzas, burritos, sodas, and ice cream. You can also bring your own food, and there are picnic tables.

GUGGENHEIM MUSEUM
1071 5th Ave. (at 89th St.)

● ●

☎ General Information: 423-3500
Museum Offices: 423-3600

🚇 4,5,6 to 86th St.

Hours:
Sun-Wed: 10 AM - 6 PM;
Fri & Sat: 10 AM - 8 PM;
Closed Thu

Admission:
Adults - $8; Students & Seniors - $5;
Kids under 12 - Free w/adult.
Friday: 6 - 8 PM, admission is pay as you wish.
Note: Strollers not permitted; baby carriers
are available at the checkroom.

Originally called the Museum of Non-Objective
Painting, the Guggenheim was founded in 1939 for
the purpose of collecting and exhibiting abstract
art. This focus has broadened over the last 60
years to encompass the many schools of twenti-
eth century art. The collection includes works
from the Impressionist, Cubist, Surrealist and
Abstract Expressionist periods to the Minimalist
and Conceptual art of the sixties and seventies.
As you walk through the spiraling galleries of this
landmark Frank Lloyd Wright building, you'll come
across works by Kandinsky, Mondrian, Degas,
Gauguin, Toulouse-Lautrec, Picasso, and Warhol,
among many others.

The Guggenheim offers a full schedule of family
programs, performances, tours, and workshops,
as well as free "Family Activity Guides" that focus
on the current special exhibitions. Information can
be obtained by calling the museum or by inquiring
at the ground-floor information desk.

MUSEUM CAFE

at the Guggenheim Musuem

 427-5682

Hours:
Fri-Tue: 9 AM - 6 PM
Thu: 9 AM - 3 PM
Brunch: No

▬ $ **Entertainment:** Museum

Note: The cafe has two entrances, one is separate from the Museum.

Run by Dean & Deluca, the cafe is adjacent to the lobby. Its spare modern design features gray walls lined with simply framed photographs chronicling the life of the of the Guggenheim. A classy cafeteria where diners bring their trays to black stone tables with stainless steel legs surrounded by modern bentwood chairs, it gets quite noisy and you may have to act fast to get a table at lunchtime. Kids may also find most of the food selections too fancy. There are, though, sand-wiches like ham and cheese, turkey, and roast beef; chicken ($4.95) and pasta ($3.95) plates; soups, salads, and fruit cups. Better yet, stop here for dessert. There is a nice range of brownies, cheese-cakes, pies and cakes ($2.95 - $3.95 per serving), as well as ice cream. Beverages are juice, soda, coffee and tea, and wine. Everything is Dean & Deluca high quality, and the prices are not unreasonable for a museum location.

If you don't mind traveling a few blocks, we suggest the following nearby places:

BARKING DOG LUNCHEONETTE 1678 3rd Ave.
(at 94th St.) 831-1800

BROTHER JIMMY'S BAIT SHACK 1644 3rd Ave.
(at 92nd St.) 426-2020

E.A.T. CAFE 1064 Madison Ave.
(between 80th & 81st Sts.) 772-0022

JACKSON HOLE 1270 Madison Ave.
(at 91st St.) 427-2820

SARABETH'S 1295 Madison Ave.
(between 92nd & 93rd Sts.) 410-7335

SOFIA 1022 Madison Ave.
(at 79th St.) 734-2676

TWINS 1712 2nd Ave.
(between 88th & 89th Sts.) 987-1111

VINEGAR FACTORY RESTAURANT 431 E. 91st St.
(between 1st & York Aves.) 987-0885

YURA & CO. 1645 3rd Ave.
(at 92nd St.) 860-8060

METROPOLITAN MUSEUM OF ART
5th Ave. & 82nd St.

● ●

☏ Information Line: 535-7710
  Main Line: 879-5500

TRANSPORTATION:

🚇 4,5,6 to 86th St.

Museum Garage: 5th Ave. and 80th St.
Validate parking tickets at the Uris Center
Information Desk. Fee.

Hours: (Some galleries open at 11 AM)
Sun, Tue-Thu: 9:30 AM - 5:15 PM
Fri & Sat: 9:30 AM - 8:45 PM
Closed Mon

Admission: Adults $8; Seniors & Students $4;
Members & Children under 12 w/adult free

Note: Strollers permitted except for Sunday
and most special exibitions; back carriers
available at 81st St. entrance

Note: Handicap entrances:
5th Ave. and 81st St. or museum garage

The grande dame of American art museums,
the Met has increased its collection from an initial
174 paintings at its founding in 1870 to over three
million works of art today. It is impossible for even
the most determined enthusiast to see everything in one day, so we suggest you concentrate
on a few select galleries you think your children
would enjoy. Our recommendation: First consider
viewing the current special exhibitions, for which
there is no extra charge, but they are popular, so
go early or on weekdays so your kids can have the
room to enjoy them.

Are your kids into *Indiana Jones* or knights in shin-
ing armor? Then the Met's first floor is the place

to begin. Go to the right from the Great Hall to the large Egyptian Wing, which includes more than one sphinx and the entire Temple of Dendur, a gift to the people of the United States from the Egyptian government in 1978. To find the Arms and Armor room, go out the door behind the temple, through most of the American Wing and look for the entrance on your left. The Greek and Roman room is to the left of the Great Hall. The Costume Institute, with over 35,000 frocks in perfect condition, displayed in periodic exhibitions, will appeal to any young fashion types in your family. The Costume Institute is located on the ground (lower) floor; to get there, use the north stairs down from the Egyptian Wing.

The museum conducts regular free programs for families with kids age six to 12. These include tours, workshops, films, and the terrific "Art Hunts" discovery guides designed to make the Met kid-friendly. These guides, along with the Met floor plan and the calendar, which lists current exhibits, programs, and family activities, are all available free in the Great Hall.

The Met has one large dining area that is a madhouse on weekends, yet during the week it is so empty that you'll feel like you own it. Accessible through the Greek and Roman room to the left of the Great Hall, it is really three restaurants in one.

MUSEUM RESTAURANT
Metropolitan Museum of Art

 570-3964

Hours:
Lunch:
Tue-Fri: 11:30 AM - 3 PM
Dinner:
Sun, Tue-Thu: 5 - 10 PM
Fri & Sat: 5 - 8 PM
Brunch:
Sat & Sun: 11:30 AM - 3 PM

 $$$ **Entertainment:** Museum

Those of you who visited the Met prior to 1982 may remember this as where the fountain with the Nymphs used to be. Now the setting, down a few steps from the entrance, is a slightly formal restaurant with linen-covered tables. If you haven't made a reservation, expect to wait at least 15 minutes on weekends. The American and Continental cuisine here is expensive ($13 to $17 entrees), and we can't think of a reason to eat here with kids.

MUSEUM BAR & CAFE

Metropolitan Museum of Art

(879-5500

Hours:
Sun, Tue - Thu:
11:30 AM - 4:30 PM
Fri & Sat: 11:30 AM - 8:30 PM
Brunch: No

$-$$ **Entertainment:** Museum

Tucked into the right-hand corner of this large room, the Bar & Cafe offers some of what's available in the cafeteria (but at higher prices) and fancier sandwiches like ham and Brie or smoked salmon rosette with cucumber salsa. There is a small bar that serves the usual beverages, delicious cappuccino, and some nice wines. On weekends you will have to wait a few minutes for one of the cafe tables. The only reason to eat here with kids is if the adults feel that they need a drink....

MUSEUM CAFETERIA
Metropolitan Museum of Art

📞 879-5500

Hours:
Breakfast:
Tues-Fri: 9:30 - 11 AM
Lunch:
Tue - Sun: 11 AM - 4:30 PM
Dinner:
Fri & Sat: 4:30 - 8:30 PM
Brunch: No

$ **Entertainment:** Museum

The line for this cafeteria forms to the right just past the Bar & Cafe. There is a wide selection of food, all better prepared than you'd expect. The hot entrees ($5.25 - $7.95) include quiches and pasta, and there are soups, salads, and sandwiches like chicken breast and tuna. Desserts are $1.95 to $2.50 for a piece of pie, cake, or ice cream. Milk, juice, lemonade, soda, coffee, tea, beer, and wine are available. It may take a little while to find a table on a busy weekend, so if you can swing it, we suggest that you have one member of your family scout for one or two of the small round cafe tables and as many chairs as you need.

There are also three beverage bars in the Met. All offer soft drinks, gourmet coffees, wine, and beer:

ESPRESSO & WINE BAR
Located off the 1st floor European Sculpture Court.
Hours:
Sun, Tue -Thu: 9:30 AM - 4:30 PM
Fri & Sat: 9:30 AM - 8:30 PM

GREAT HALL BALCONY BAR
Not appropriate for children.
Open Friday and Saturday evenings from 4:30 to 8:30 PM with live classical music starting at 5 PM.

ROOF SCULPTURE GARDEN
ESPRESSO & WINE BAR
Featuring great views, the roof bar is open from May through late September from 9:30 AM until 45 minutes before the museum closes. Take the elevator from the south side of the European Sculpture Court.

If you don't mind traveling a few blocks, we also suggest the following nearby places:
ANTICO CAFFE 1477 Second Ave.
(between 77th & 78th Sts.) 879-4824
E.A.T. Cafe 1064 Madison Ave.
(between 80th & 81st Sts.) 772-0022
GOOGIES ITALIAN DINER 1491 2nd Ave.
(at 78th St.) 717-1122
JACKSON HOLE 1611 2nd Ave.
(between 83rd & 84th Sts.) 737-8788
MARY ANN'S 1503 2nd Ave.
(at 78th St.) 249-6165
SARABETH'S 1295 Madison Ave.
(between 92nd & 93rd Sts.) 410-7335
SOFIA 1022 Madison Ave.
(at 79th St.) 734-2676

WHITNEY MUSEUM OF AMERICAN ART

945 Madison Ave. (at 75th St.)

• •

(General Information: 570-3676

🚇 6 to 77th St.

Hours:
Wed, Fri-Sun: 11 AM - 6 PM
Thu: 1 - 8 PM
Closed Mon & Tue
Admission: Adults $8; Seniors & Students $6; Kids under 12 Free

Admission fees waived if you plan only to eat at the restaurant. Get pass at information desk.

Founded by Gertrude Vanderbilt Whitney in 1931, this museum specializes in exhibitions of contemporary art. The permanent collection includes works by Georgia O'Keeffe, Jasper Johns, and Edward Hopper.

Although not exactly next door, the following Upper East Side restaurants are recommended:

ANTICO CAFFEE 1477 Second Ave.
(between 77th & 78th Sts.) 879-4824
BROTHER JIMMY'S BBQ 1461 1st. Ave.
(at 76th St.) 288-0999
E.A.T. Cafe 1064 Madison Ave.
(between 80th & 81st Sts.) 772-0022
EJ's LUNCHEONETTE 1271 3rd Ave.
(at 73rd St.) 472-0600
GOOGIES ITALIAN DINER 1491 2nd Ave.
(at 78th St.) 717-1122
MARY ANN'S 1503 2nd Ave.
(at 78th St.) 249-6165
SOFIA 1022 Madison Ave.
(at 79th St.) 734-2676

SARABETH'S AT THE WHITNEY

Whitney Museum of American Art

℡ 570-3676

Hours:
Tue: 12 noon - 3:30 PM
Wed-Fri: 11 AM - 4:30 PM
Sat & Sun: 10 AM - 4:30 PM
Closed Mon

Brunch:
Sat & Sun 10 AM - 4:30 PM

▭ $$-$$$ **Entertainment:** Museum

Note: Members receive 10% discount. Restrooms for the handicapped are in the museum.

A branch of Sarabeth's provides the restaurant service here. The cafe features a dramatic open ceiling and a wall of windows facing the Sculpture Courtyard. If you are planning only to visit the restaurant, you can obtain a free pass at the Whitney's information desk. Expect a wait to be seated at the simple wooden tables with uphol-stered armchairs, especially during weekend brunches. Unfortunately, the austerity of the Whitney's building does not allow for the warmth associated with the other Sarabeth's locations, despite the wonderful friendliness of the staff. The cafe here is noisy and a bit uptight; kids find it frumpy. Many kids will have difficulty finding something appealing to eat, other than the expensive desserts, and the little sandwich cart adjacent to the cafe isn't much of an alternative. The Whitney Museum is a smart place to take the kids, but we suggest you plan to feed them else-where.

UPPER WEST SIDE

. . . .

The **Upper West Side** includes the area from 59th Street to 110th Street and from the Hudson River to Central Park West.

RESTAURANTS

. . . .

ATTRACTIONS with RESTAURANTS

. . . .

BOULEVARD

2398 Broadway (at 88th St.)

📞 874-7400

🚇 1, 9 to 86th St.

Hours:
Lunch/Dinner:
Mon-Thu: 11 AM - 12 midnight
Fri: 11 AM - 1 AM
Sat: 3 PM - 1 AM
Sun: 3 PM - 12 midnight

Brunch:
Sat & Sun: 10 AM-3 PM

💳 $$

Entertainment: Crayons & paper-covered tables.

Note: Reservations recommended for Friday through Monday nights. Accessible to wheelchairs in front section only, which is also the smoking section.

If you go to eat at Boulevard on a weekend night, you will find strollers lined up outside like planes on the runway at La Guardia — this restaurant is a fave for West Side families. Boulevard is a casual restaurant with multiple levels of dining on two floors. It is suited for every age, from infant to grandparent. The bar on the ground level separates the front and back dining rooms, and in season there is a lovely sidewalk cafe. Both floors are noisy, with a lot of commotion and a ton of kids, but the upstairs, overlooking Broadway, is the quieter and we prefer it when the restaurant is busy. On slower nights we like to sit in the front (bar area). The wait is usually no longer than 15 minutes unless you have a large party, but we recommend reservations or calling ahead if you are coming here on weekends.

KIDS EAT NEW YORK

One of the reasons for the restaurant's popularity is the $5.95 children's menu. It offers burgers, dogs, chicken fingers, ribs, pasta with sauce or butter, macaroni and cheese, and grilled cheese. All come with milk, soda, juice, and ice cream. Another reason is the specials — the $11.95 early-bird blue plate special (grilled salmon, chicken, or strip steak, salad, and coffee), the daily offerings that include dinosaur (beef) ribs and shrimp, and the $15.95 Monday night Pig-Out (ribs, chicken and Rolling Rock). Pigs are the motif of this restaurant, and while barbecue is the main focus, the extensive menu offers salads, sandwiches, pasta, fish, vegetarian, and Mexican dishes. The food is basic, the service fast. And kids (the more you bring the better) are very, very welcome.

DALLAS BBQ

27 W. 72nd St.
(between Columbus Ave. & Central Park West)

☎ 873-2004
🚇 B,C,1,2,3 to 72nd St.

Hours:
Sun-Thu: 12 noon - 12 midnight
Fri & Sat: 12 noon - 1 AM
Brunch: No

💳 $ **Entertainment:** No

Among Sam's uptown pals, Dallas BBQ is high on the list. Specializing in large portions of smoky chicken, ribs, and burgers, we frequent the two uptown locations, one on the Upper East Side and one on the Upper West Side. Service is fast and friendly, and you will always see a lot of kids. The prices on the simple menu are quite low, with a BBQ half-chicken costing $5.95 and ribs $8.95. Salads and burgers range from $4.95 to $7 and a basket of fried shrimp or chicken wings will only set you back $7.95. Be seated before 6:30 PM Monday through Friday, or before 5 PM on Saturday and Sunday, and you can order two half-chicken dinners for a total of $7.95. Oversized frozen cocktails are a specialty (kids can order theirs without alcohol), and in addition to the regular sodas and milk, there is a full bar.

The West Side location is a good-sized, attractive room with mirrored columns and Indian blankets with cattle skulls, featuring a lot of black wood and high-back chairs arranged around the clean, dark tables. Please note that we recommend only the two uptown locations of this chain. The two downtown branches on University Place and St. Mark's Place do not, we feel, represent the same dining experience.

Upper East Side location: 1265 3rd Ave. (between 72nd & 73rd Sts.) 772-9393

EJ'S LUNCHEONETTE

477 Amsterdam Ave.

(between 81st & 82nd Sts.)

(873-3444

🚇 1, 9 to 79th St.;
B, C to 81st St.

Hours:
Mon-Thu: 8 AM - 11 PM
Fri & Sat: 8 AM - 12 midnight
Sun: 8 AM - 10:30 PM
Breakfast/Brunch: Anytime

 $-$$ **Entertainment:** No

We liked the bright shiny atmosphere of EJ's as soon as we walked in. The booths, tin ceilings, 1940s advertisements, and old-fashioned ice cream counter all say family diner, and each of the three locations of this New York favorite is clearly kid-friendly. We are always greeted with a smile, and the cheerful staff never seems to have a problem with pint-sized diners who drop forks, spill milk, and generally make a little more noise than their parents would prefer. What is unexpected is how good the food is. The blue plate specials (served on blue plates) always feature several fish dinners, pastas, soups, and salads.

There is a special kids' menu that includes pancakes, French toast, eggs; burgers, tuna melts, PB&J, grilled cheese, and pasta, plain or with sauce. There are also a lot of dishes on the main menu that appeal to both kids and adults. Several youngsters that we know say this is their favorite restaurant.

As breakfast is served any time, half the menu is devoted to a wide variety of flapjacks, waffles, eggs, and omelets. For drinks, kids can choose from milk, juice, soda, and milk shakes. (Beer, wine, coffee and tea are also available for grown-ups.) And for the clean-plate club, there are rewards of cakes, brownies, pies, and ice cream.

Sam likes the fact that the waiters really listen to his requests, especially the one for "no green stuff!" He also appreciates the quick service, that it's OK to be a little noisy, and that you don't have to be perfect at dinner, because, after all, EJ's is a diner.

Other locations:
Upper East Side: 1271 3rd Ave.
(at 73rd St.) 472-0600
Greenwich Village: 432 6th Ave.
(between 9th and 10th Sts.) 473-5555

ERNIE'S

2150 Broadway (between 75th & 76th Sts.)

(496-1588

🚇 2,3 to 72nd St.;
1,9 to 79th St

Hours:
Mon-Fri: 12 noon - 11:30 PM
Sat & Sun: 11:30 AM - 11:30 PM
Brunch:
Sat & Sun: 11:30 AM - 4 PM

▬ $$ **Entertainment::** No

Note: Kids' menu only at brunch

One of the first cavernous-style restaurants in
New York, where the music of the moment is the
collective din of many conversations, Ernie's has
been drawing diners for more than 14 years.
The delicious family-style New American/Italian
cuisine is served in a setting that reminds us of
trendy LA restaurants. Yet the ambiance at
Ernie's is quite casual, and noisy kids will never
be noticed. Especially popular with families is the
weekend brunch, when the $5.25 children's menu
offers pizza, spaghetti, squiggly macaroni and
cheese, burgers, chicken tenders, and breakfast
dishes, all served with a beverage. During other
hours, kids can order burgers, pizzas, and half
orders of pasta.

The large main menu has classic Italian dishes
prepared with an American twist. Ernie's is known
for its angel hair pasta with lobster and aspara-
gus in a creamy tomato sauce, grilled and roasted

chicken, and Caesar salad. The large portions are served family-style — plan to share or else to take home what's left.

The high-ceilinged space has been loosely divided into a cafe/bar area in front and a much larger dining room in the rear, with exposed brick and antiqued linen-colored walls. Diners are seated in comfy oak chairs at well-spaced tables. The back wall of windows overlooks the winterized garden dining area, which is a favorite for families. We think Ernie's is a good place for a special, yet not too formal, family meal. The food is tasty, the service welcoming and swift.

GOOD ENOUGH TO EAT

483 Amsterdam Ave.
(between 83rd & 84th Sts.)

📞 496-0163

🚇 1,9, to 86th St.;
C to 86th St.

Hours:
Breakfast:
Mon-Fri: 8 AM - 4 PM
Sat & Sun: 9 AM - 4 PM
Lunch: 11:30 AM - 4 PM daily
Dinner:
Mon-Sat: 6 - 10:30 PM
Sun: 6 - 10 PM

Brunch: Sun: Breakfast menu
9 AM to 4 PM (No reservations)

💳 $-$$ **Entertainment:** Monday nights:
The "Singing Dad" performs

Note: No kids' menu but half portions may be ordered for kids

Good Enough to Eat is a cozy little country cafe in the heart of Manhattan. Owner Carrie Levin, a mother of three young boys herself, practices an "extended concept of cooking and eating" in a setting filled with rustic charm. As you pass through the exterior barn doors, the first thing you may notice is the picket fence separating the small barn-board bar from the dining area. Bouquets of fresh wildflowers are set out on the oak tables, many of which are made out of old sewing machine bases. The walls are decorated with pretty quilts and a collection of rakes, baskets, pepper mills, pressed tin figures, and a lot of cow ornaments. Cows are a sort of logo here, and they're everywhere.

The farm-oriented menu has a lot on it for kids to choose from. We suggest their roasted half chicken, the grilled pork chops with apple-onion topping and sweet potato fries, or the popular meatloaf dinner which comes with mashed potatoes, peas, and carrots. Kid favorites also include macaroni and cheese, homemade pizzas, regular and veggie burgers, and fish and chips. The daily specials are worth considering, such as the chilled potato and arugula soup, the spinach lasagna made with sun-dried tomatoes and three cheeses, and the chicken and wild rice salad with vegetables, served over baby greens. There is also a selection of homemade desserts, and, if you love what you eat here, you can buy a copy of the restaurant's cookbook to try its recipes at home.

Infants in strollers are welcome and the staff is friendly to kids of all ages. Storybooks are available for entertainment, but we recommend that you bring cards or coloring books.

ISOLA

485 Columbus Ave. (between 83rd & 84th Sts.)

(362-7400

🚊 B,C,1,9 to 86th St.

Hours:
Lunch: 12 noon - 4 PM
Dinner:
Mon- Fri: 5 - 11:30 PM
Sat: 4 PM - 12 midnight
Sun: 4 - 11 PM
Brunch:
Sat & Sun: 12 noon - 4 PM

▬ $-$$ **Entertainment:** No

For us, part of what makes a trip to the American Museum of Natural History special is a visit to Isola for lunch or dinner. Isola means "island" in Italian and refers to Sicily, the homeland of the owner's family. The cuisine is a combination of well-prepared fish, wonderful pastas, and brick oven pizza — all great choices for kids and adults. Fortunately, the staff loves to see kids, including infants, here.

Open since 1991, Isola has a casual hip sophistication, with a late-evening scene that can really heat up. Reservations are not usually necessary, however, for lunch or early dinner. The room itself is stylishly spare and can seat about 80 diners. The dark yellow walls are randomly stenciled with images of the sea, and the gray marble floor, brown marble cafe tables, and simple black chairs complement the small handsome bar. A busy sidewalk cafe is open in season, protected from traffic by small fences topped with pretty flower boxes.

Whether you choose from appetizers such as shrimp with fennel and olives, or the salads including homemade mozzarella with roasted tomatoes and peppers, the food is wonderful. Isola is known for its fresh pastas, made on the premises, including the black linguine made from squid ink (served with a red shrimp sauce) and its raviolis. Although it's not mentioned on the menu, the kitchen is happy to make half orders of pastas for kids. Sam prefers to order pizza, which he likes to watch being prepared in the wood-burning oven in the rear of the restaurant. Entrees include chicken, steak, veal chops, and fish. The prices are very good for food of this quality, with the pastas and pizzas averaging $11, and the entrees just a little more.

JACKSON HOLE

517 Columbus Ave. (at 85th St.)

(362-5177

🚊 B,C,1,9 to 86th St.

<u>Hours:</u>
Mon-Thu: 7 AM- 1 AM
Fri: 7 AM - 4 AM
Sat: 8 AM - 4 AM
Sun: 8 AM - 12 midnight

Brunch:
Sat & Sun: 8 AM - 3 PM

  AMEX only **$** **Entertainment:** No

    6+

Note: The rest rooms can accommodate wheel-chairs but do not have railings

Immensely popular with kids, the five locations of Jackson Hole are all pretty much the same, varying mostly in size. Our favorites are 64th Street on the East Side and Columbus Avenue on the West Side. Decorated with old metal Coke signs, snowshoes, and black and white Old West photos, these restaurants can get a little rowdy, especially as the evening progresses. We generally choose a table in the rear of one of the dining rooms, which are furnished with butcher block tables under hanging Tiffany-style lamps.

The staff is very friendly to kids and courteous about cleaning up spills. There is a good children's menu with items such as burgers, chicken breast on a bun, chili, tuna sandwiches, and grilled cheese, for $3.50 to $5, including fries and a drink. The menu sheet is also a small activity page.

The regular menu is enormous, with around 200 listed items, including 39 types of beef or turkey burgers and an equal number of varieties of the house's special marinated chicken. With all the appetizers, salads, sandwiches, omelets, Mexican food, and blue plate specials, your biggest dilemma of the evening may be choosing what to eat. Sodas, shakes, milk, juice, beer, wine and coffee are available. We suggest you try the Jackson Hole brand root beer which is served with its own frosty mug. For dessert, try the waffles or ice creams, pies, and cakes.

Other locations:
Midtown: 521 3rd Ave.
(at 35th St.) 679-3264
Upper East Side: 232 E. 64th St.
(between 2nd & 3rd Aves.) 371-7187
Upper East Side: 1611 2nd Ave.
(between 83rd & 84th Sts.) 737-8788
Upper East Side: 1270 Madison Ave.
(at 91st St.) 427-2820

JOHN'S PIZZERIA

48 W. 65th St.
(between Central Park W & Columbus Ave.)

☎ 721-7001
🚇 1,9 to 66th St.

<u>Hours:</u>
11:30 AM - 11:30 PM
Brunch: No

 $

Entertainment:
Watching the pizzas being made

Many kids and adults alike rate John's as the best pizza in New York City. Partly it's because the thin-crust pizza is really terrific, but it's also because the friendly helter-skelter activity makes every-one feel right at home. There are 54 varieties of pizza, as well as pastas and salads. Despite the famous "no slices" policy, these pies are so fabulous that customers keep coming back for more. All four locations feature their trademark coal-fired brick ovens, and when kids go over to watch their pizzas being made, the chefs really ham it up. Expect a wait if you go at peak dining times, but even that will be worth it because of the staff's great attitude and the spectacular New York "fold-over"-style pizza (so-called because the best way to manage a slice is to fold it lengthwise). Beverages are beer, wine, and soda. There are no desserts.

John's at Lincoln Center sports a classier uptown look, with its spacious two-level loft design, oak decor, and bar area, yet it still maintains all the friendliness of the other locations.

Other locations: (See reviews.)

Greenwich Village: 278 Bleecker St. (between 6th & 7th Aves.) 243-1680

Midtown: 260 W. 44th St. (between Broadway & 8th Ave.)
Note: Telephone number not available as of press time.

Upper East Side: 408 E. 64th St. (between 1st & York Aves.) 935-2895

MAIN STREET

446 Columbus Ave. (between 81st & 82nd Sts.)

(873-5025

🚇 1,9 to 79th St.

Hours:
Mon: 5:30 - 10 PM
Tue-Thu: 5:30 - 11 PM
Fri: 5:30 PM - 12 midnight
Sat: 5 PM - 12 midnight
Sun: 5 - 10 PM

Brunch:
Sat & Sun: 11:30 AM - 3 PM

▬ $$ **Entertainment:** Crayons and paper on the tables

Bring your family and your appetite when you visit Main Street, where the delicious food is served family style. Of the salads, our favorite is the Country Inn Salad, made from assorted greens, tomatoes, goat cheese, bacon, and walnuts. The giant appetizers include a version of sushi hand rolls (tuna, vegetables and wasabi in a tortilla)

and grilled portobello mushrooms. Entrees that we recommend are whole roasted chicken served with a mound of shoestring fries, meatloaf, roasted turkey prepared with a raisin, walnut, and pecan cornbread stuffing, and pepper steak served with wonderful mashed potatoes. (Mashed potatoes also can be ordered as an all-you-can-eat side dish for $7.50.) Pasta choices range from tricolored fusilli and seafood linguine to vegetable lasagna and wild mushroom ravioli. Portions are sized so that a family of five might be satisfied with a salad, a main course, and a pasta dish. I have also seen families of three or four order a salad and the deep dish chicken pot pie.

A separate children's menu offers single kid-sized servings of macaroni and cheese, spaghetti and meatballs, fried chicken, bite-sized franks, and grilled cheese. Desserts include apple pie à la mode, brownies with ice cream and chocolate topping, and chocolate mousse with raspberry sauce.

The restaurant is difficult to locate on the street — look for the large blue awning. The dining room, reached by walking past the handsome front bar and down a hallway lined with old family photos, is an atrium with a high glass roof, brick walls, green curtains. Small centerpiece planters on each of the tables continue the greenhouse theme. An excellent choice for family get-togethers, Main Street is ideal for a large or small group.

MARY ANN'S

2452 Broadway (at 91st St.)

☎ 877-0132

🚇 1,2,3,9 to 96th St.

Hours:
Lunch Mon-Fri: 12 noon - 4 PM
Dinner:
Mon-Thu: 4 - 10:30 PM
Fri & Sat: 4 - 11:30 PM
Sun: 4 - 10 PM

Brunch:
Sat & Sun: 12 noon - 4 PM

▬ No AMEX **\$-\$\$ Entertainment:** Toy Box

 6+

Note: Sometimes on Fridays & Saturdays there are mariachi bands starting at 8 PM; call to confirm.

Mary Ann's, with four locations in Manhattan, is an ideal choice for good traditional Mexican fare at modest prices. With its "La Bamba" music, handmade tiles and stucco walls, punched tin star-shaped lamps, and Mexican blankets, you almost feel like you're in Tijuana. Be sure to go early — by 8:15 PM, every table will be filled and there will be a crowd at the bar waiting to eat.

First thing, Sam dives into the bottomless bowl of free chips and salsa. The homemade guacamole starter is served in a stone cornmeal grinder. The \$3.95 kids' menu provides large servings of tacos, enchiladas, cheese quesadillas, chicken fajitas, or crispy flauta chicken rolls, all with rice, beans, or French fries. All the other dishes are ample, too — we never leave hungry.

KIDS EAT NEW YORK

The sizzling fajitas, available in steak, chicken or vegetarian variations, served with a lot of fanfare, are probably the most popular dish on the menu, but you really can't go wrong with any of the classic Mexican combination plates. We have especially enjoyed the Santa Fe sirloin burritos, the taco and enchilada specials, and the Mary Ann's combo, a shrimp burrito and chicken tostado. Vegetarian varieties are also available. For something a little different, try the *camarones Veracruz*, a delicious preparation of sautéed jumbo shrimp. Like most of the other dishes, these are served with generous sides of rice, beans, and salad.

Other locations:

Chelsea: 116 8th Ave.
(at 16th St.) 633-0877

East Village: 80 2nd Ave.
(at 5th St.) 475-5939

Upper East Side: 1503 2nd Ave.
(at 78th St.) 249-6165 (See review.)

MIMI'S MACARONI

718 Amsterdam Ave. (at 95th St.)

☎ 866-6311

🚇 1,2,3,9,C to 96th St.

Hours:
Lunch: 11:30 AM - 4 PM
Dinner: 4 - 11:30 PM
Early Bird Special: 4 - 5:45 PM
Brunch: Sundays only:
11:30 AM - 4 PM

▬ No AMEX **$$** **Entertainment:** Yes

We wish there were more restaurants like this in Manhattan. Going to Mimi's Macaroni is like visiting your favorite aunt's house. From the moment you arrive, the owner and the staff go out of their way to make you feel happy and right at home. As you go to be seated, you pass a large inviting box filled with toys to take to the table. The dining room itself is not very big (it seats approximately 60 people) and has a cozy feel to it. White wainscoting meets a deep cobalt blue halfway up the walls, and tall windows overlook the street. The dining tables are paper-covered, so bring your colored pencils and markers.

Mimi's Macaroni is named after the owner's daughter, who was three years old when the restaurant opened in 1994. If you go for an early dinner, you are sure to meet her. The place was designed to be kid-friendly, and it seems as if every other table is occupied by families. There is (of course) a good children's menu, with each dish named after one of Mimi's cousins and all priced

293

at $4.50. Kids can choose from spaghetti with meatballs, chicken parmigiana, chicken cutlet with pasta, fettuccine Alfredo, baked ziti, and ravioli. And don't worry about fidgety kids who can't manage to keep their silverware on the table — the friendly staff in this nice and noisy restaurant will be happy to get you more.

All the dishes we adults have ordered have been well prepared, including rigatoni with wild mushrooms, capellini with roasted artichokes, freshly-made pappardelle in tomato sauce, and the fresh ravioli. We've also enjoyed sautéed chicken Maria and grilled salmon in a garlic butter sauce. Desserts include Tiramisu, cannolis, and ice cream. There are milk, sodas, and a full bar.

At the end of your meal, the owner will come around to ask you to play a quick game of "Tumbling." If you or someone in your party (only one guess per table) correctly identifies the number that shakes out of a cone-shaped tumbler, your entire table's meal will be free.

MUSEUM CAFE

366 Columbus Ave. (at 77th St.)

(799-0150

1,9 to 79th/Broadway;
2,3 to 72nd St.

Hours:
Mon-Thu: 11:30 AM - 12 midnight
Fri: 11:30 AM - 1 AM
Sat: 11 AM - 1 AM
Sun: 11 AM - 12 midnight

Brunch: (No reservations)
Sat & Sun: 11 AM - 4:15 PM

$$ **Entertainment:** Crayons, butcher paper on tables

The Museum Cafe is a pretty little restaurant located across Columbus Avenue from the American Museum of Natural History. It's a nice casual place for lunch or dinner, especially in conjunction with viewing the dinosaurs or a special exhibit. The sunny front greenhouse with French cafe chairs is our favorite place to sit. The cozy dining room is also pleasant, a combination of exposed bricks, burnt yellow wainscoting trimmed in Chesapeake blue, and ecru walls. A few Beaux Arts posters add a decorative accent. The upscale neighborhood clientele is relaxed about kids. Busy on the weekends, the restaurant can be quite quiet during the week.

The tables are covered with butcher paper over linens, each with a jar of crayons. There is a $4.95 kids' selection of chicken fingers with fries, pasta and butter, ravioli with tomato sauce, macaroni and cheese, grilled cheese sandwiches or muffin pizzas. Also on the kids' menu are a few museum-related puzzles. The Museum Burger with fries

295

is also a good choice, as are the sandwiches and salads such as Greek with chicken or the warm goat cheese over greens with balsamic vinegar. Our experience with the entrees, however, has been disappointing — we found the crab cakes bland and the fried chicken merely average. The service, however, is welcoming, and since both the owners and the manager are parents of small children, they understand kids. We recommend the weekend brunch.

NOVA GRILL

2330 Broadway (at 85th St.)

(579-5100

🚇 1,9,B,C to 86th St.

Hours:
Lunch: 11:30 AM - 4:30 PM
Dinner:
Sun-Thu: 5 - 11 PM
Fri & Sat: 5 PM - 12 midnight
Brunch: No

▬ $$$ **Entertainment:** No

Note: No kids' menu but will do special orders. Reservations recommended

One of the great things about New York is discovering fabulous new things just by walking down the street. That's what we were doing when we found the Nova Grill. Its sophisticated modern architecture, a type common in TriBeCa or in the Flatiron district, wasn't at all what we expected on the Upper West Side. The restaurant had only been open for about six weeks when we discovered it, but we rounded up a group of friends and went back later that day for a most enjoyable dinner.

The cavernous two-story restaurant has plastered adobe-colored walls, a dark lattice ceiling that shelters recessed lighting behind wire mesh, and an enormous burnished copper exhaust pipe that reminds us of the film *Brazil*. The first floor is a bar area and a large dining room that's great for people watching. Up the grand staircase is an even larger dining room with wonderful windows overlooking the street.

The chef, J. P. Richards, who has worked at America and the Sequoia Grill in Washington, DC, has put together a menu emphasizing grilled or wood-roasted vegetables, meats, and fish. It includes seared yellowfin tuna steak, rigatoni with grilled asparagus and chevre, and grilled veal chops with a caramelized shallot sauce. There are equally interesting appetizers (the mussels in linquicia sausage broth is memorable), soups (such as the roasted tomato), and salads. The staff bends over backward to please kids, who should not miss the pizzas prepared in a wood-fired oven; they also can order half portions of pasta and the kitchen will prepare any entree to their specifications, including "plain."

Our favorite dessert is chocolate soufflé: a custard-cup-sized portion of brownie-crusted mousse with a thick hot fudge center. It comes with a scoop of toffee malted milk ice cream and a large, thin sugar cookie made with white chocolate. Because the entrees are rather high ($16 to $20), we suggest that dinner here be reserved for celebrations. The winning combination of the food, the service, and the ambiance, however, will make any occasion special.

OLLIE'S NOODLE SHOP & GRILLE
2315 Broadway (at 84th St.)
362-3712
1,9 to 86th St.

OLLIE'S NOODLE SHOP & GRILLE
2957 Broadway (at 116th St.)
932-3300
1,9 to 116th St.

Hours:
Sun-Thu: 11:30 AM - 12 midnight
Fri & Sat: 11:30 AM - 1 AM
Sun: 11:30 AM - 11:30 PM

■ $ **Entertainment::** No

More than just a noodle shop, Ollie's offers tasty westernized versions of Cantonese, Mandarin, and Szechuan dishes. The extensive menu, with more than 200 items, has something for everyone, including plain grilled chicken and beef, and fish. One child we know won't try Chinese but loved Ollie's tuna kabob. (We make sure the sauces come "on the side.") The dumplings have a loyal following, as do the scallion pancakes and the lemon chicken. Prices are very reasonable, and the portions are large — order only one dish for each person and share. Beverages include sodas, beer and wine and there is a pot of Chinese tea on every table. The service is adequate, you don't have to ask for chopsticks, and fortune cookies appear right before you leave.

PATSY'S PIZZERIA

64 W. 74th St. (at Columbus Ave.)

☎ 579-3000

🚇 1,2,3,9, B,C to 72nd St.

Hours:

Sun-Thu: 12 noon - 11 PM

Fri & Sat: 12 noon - 12 midnight

Brunch: No

 \$-\$\$ Entertainment: No

In the first quarter of this century, several young Italian pizza chefs, including John of John's Pizzeria, Tottono of Coney Island, and Patsy Lancieri, learned their craft at Gennaro Lombardi's restaurant. These chefs then went on to open their own, now famous, pizzerias. The one Patsy Lancieri opened in 1933 in East Harlem is still in business, serving not only pizza but also salads, soups, pastas, and desserts. His nephew, Patsy Grimaldi, subsequently went on to open Patsy Grimaldi's. Recently, four branches of Patsy's Pizzeria have opened in Manhattan, all of which we recommend for families.

Patsy's Pizzeria offers brick-oven pizzas and an extensive menu that includes appetizers, salads, and pasta. The pizza ovens are in the dining rooms, where you can watch the chefs at work. Pizzas cost \$10.95 and \$12.95 and toppings are an additional \$2 each. Sam says that "this is the kind of pizza that everyone should make. First they put the cheese on the dough, then the tomato sauce. That way, some of the sauce goes in the cheese,

299

some on top of it, and some under it."
The West Side Patsy's, with its green marble
tables and brick walls, is a very pleasant place to
enjoy these great pizzas. The small pizza is certainly big enough for two kids.

Salads and pastas are also available in individual
and family-sized portions. Roughly twice the price
of the generous single servings, the "big bowl" family orders are an excellent buy, easily serving a
family of four. The staff is friendly and upbeat.

Other locations: (See reviews.)
Murray Hill: 509 3rd Ave.
(at 34th St.) 689-7500
Greenwich Village: 67 University Pl.
(between 10th & 11th Sts.) 533-3500
Upper East Side: 1312 2nd Ave.
(at 69th St.) 639-1000

POPOVER CAFE

551 Amsterdam Avenue
(between 86th & 87th Sts.)

☎ 595-8555
🚇 1,9,B,C to 86th St.

Hours:
Breakfast:
Mon-Fri: 8 - 11:30 AM
Lunch: 11:30 AM - 3 PM
Daily Sandwich/Salad/Soup
menu: 3 - 5 PM
Dinner:
Sun-Thu: 3 - 10 PM
Fri & Sat: 3 - 11 PM
Brunch:
Sat & Sun: 9 AM - 3 PM

💳 $-$$ **Entertainment:** No

Popover Cafe is a cute, comfortable family eatery, and the perfect place to take grandparents. Old gilt-framed mirrors decorate the ecru walls, along with Victorian brass lamps with frosted milkglass shades. Kids are allowed to roam about here, visiting the teddy bears tucked in various windows and corners. The place itself also seems to wander all around with little dining areas on slightly varying levels that create an open, yet intimate, sense of dining. You may have to wait ten or 15 minutes, but once seated, the service is welcoming and quick.

Popovers are the specialty, and are prepared here in a number of ways — from classic breakfast and dessert types to a wide selection of sandwiches (served with a side order of pasta salad). We suggest that you try a popover sandwich (they are also available on more traditional breads) such as

301

the Sorry Charlie (tuna with avocado, tomatoes, sprouts, and melted cheddar), or the Sweet William (black forest ham, sliced pear, melted gruyere and Russian dressing). Eggs all come with popovers and are prepared in a wide variety of ways, including "shirred" (baked in an au gratin dish), and the unusual Cappuccino Eggs (steamed fluffy with a cappuccino jet). There are delicious salads, soups, burgers and pastas (try the smoked salmon fettuccine) available from 11 AM on. Entrees include Cornish game hen with cous-cous, grilled marinated chicken on wild greens with toasted pecans, pears, and a blue-cheese vinaigrette, and pork loin medallions with honey, ginger and blackberries.

A simple children's menu offers peanut butter sandwiches for $2.95 and grilled cheese, pasta, and burgers for $3.50. Kids can choose milk shakes, sodas, lemonade or juice. We like the coffees, teas, or specialty drinks such as Belgian cocoa or Orzata (steamed milk with almond syrup). There is a full bar.

SARABETH'S

423 Amsterdam Ave.
(between 80th & 81st Sts.)

📞 496-6280
🚇 1,9 to 79th St.;
   B,C to 81st St.

Hours:
Breakfast:
Mon-Fri: 8 AM - 3:30 PM
Lunch:
Mon-Fri: 11 AM - 3:30 PM
Tea: 4 - 5 PM
Dinner:
Mon-Thu: 6 - 10 PM
Fri & Sat: 6 - 11 PM
Sun: 6 - 9:30 PM

Brunch:
Sat & Sun: 9 AM - 4 PM

💳 $$-$$$ Entertainment: No

Note: Reservations accepted for dinner only and are strongly recommended

Both of the Sarabeth's started out as bakeries — first on the West Side and later on the East Side. Later still, the Sarabeth's Cafe at the Whitney Museum was opened (see review).

Despite the high menu prices (appetizers average $7, dinner entrees $17), the restaurants continue to be popular because the food is skillfully prepared with quality ingredients. Sarabeth's serves a lot of children even though there is no kids' menu, probably because the comfortable ambiance suits diners of all ages. In fact, the West Side location has a sign for stroller parking. Unfortunately, neither restaurant takes brunch reservations, so you may have to wait for a table.

KIDS EAT NEW YORK

The amiable staff does a good job of remembering regulars. The menu changes daily and is slightly different for each location. The smooth, buttery tomato soup and the crab cakes with baby greens are two of the appetizers that I most enjoy. We recommend the chicken pot pie with crispy cooked vegetables in a light pastry crust, the roasted red pepper and mozzarella ravioli in a fresh tomato sauce, and the grilled lamb with roasted potatoes. Even though we clean our plates, we always sample Sarabeth's incredible desserts (fruit tarts, chocolate cakes, melt-in-your-mouth brownies). But if you can't even contemplate the thought of another bite, you can purchase these baked goods to take home.

Other location:
Upper East Side: 1295 Madison Ave.
(between 92nd & 93rd Sts.) 410-7335

TAVERN ON THE GREEN

Central Park West at 67th St.

☎ 873-3200

🚇 1,9 to 66th St/Lincoln Center;
B,C to 72nd St.

Hours:
Lunch:
Mon-Fri: 11:30 AM - 3:30 PM
Pre-theatre menu Sun-Fri:
5:30 - 6:30 PM
Dinner:
Sun: 5 - 10:30 PM
Mon-Sat: 5 - 11:30 PM

Brunch:
Sat & Sun: 10 AM - 3:30 PM

💳 $$$$ **Entertainment:**
Menu coloring; gift shop

Note: Valet parking available: Two hours: $7.50; Additional hours: $2 each. Tip: $2 minimum. For garden dining, reservations are accepted only on day of dining. Semiformal dress

Tavern on the Green used to seem like a terribly expensive, frumpy place that attracted tourists by the busload. Well, it's still expensive, and still filled with tourists, but as we walked under the long awning to the front door, our trepidation disappeared. By the time we were seated, Sam was positively giddy with excitement.

The setting has a fairy-tale quality that enchants children and adults alike. Built in 1870, the central building once housed sheep that grazed in Sheeps Meadow. By 1934, the herd had been moved to Brooklyn and the Victorian Gothic structure had been converted into a restaurant, which existed for 40 years, until it was closed for renovation.

KIDS EAT NEW YORK

Two years and ten million dollars later, Tavern on the Green reopened as a glittering palace with vaulted ceilings, baroque fixtures, and lavish decorations including many, many chandeliers with flickering candles. The Crystal Room also opened in 1976, with its now-famous windowed walls and ceiling, and lacquered Easter-egg yellow columns with white filigreed detail.

We love the hall of mirrors leading from the front vestibule to the dining rooms, with its life-sized statues of deer and bears. The Crystal Room, with pink damask-covered tables surrounded by big white chairs, feels more like Disneyland than the center of Manhattan. Sunsets viewed from the Crystal Room can be magical. Outside, splendid little lights outline the Tavern's buildings and encircle the branches of the surrounding trees. Visible also is a topiary zoo, bordering the outdoor dining patio. When you visit, look for a seal balancing a ball on its nose, a tusked elephant, a horse with a flying mane, and King Kong.

Unfortunately, even with the arrival of world-class executive chef Patrick Clark, the food is inconsistent. For that reason, it's best to stick to the least complicated dishes on the menu. Good choices are the roasted chicken, the tender grilled filet mignon with merlot sauce, or the veal t-bone with green beans and mashed potatoes. The Norwegian salmon with a fennel seed crust is delicious but sinfully rich in a reduced butter sauce. We loved the creamy lobster bisque, but the penne Bolognese was too salty. Skip the flavorless gluey risotto and the bland and mushy tuna carpaccio. Entrees run a steep $23 to $32, with soups, salads, and appetizers ranging from $6.50 to $15. The desserts can also be hit or miss. The ice cream Oreo cookie is fabulous, with layers of solid chocolate, chocolate cake, and vanilla, chocolate and toffee ice creams served in a lake of white and dark chocolate sauce. The classic crème brûlée, on the other hand, was so runny we sent it back to the kitchen.

The new children's menu doubles as a coloring activity sheet. (Crayons are provided.) Children can choose among chicken on skewers with buttered rice, meatloaf, grilled shrimp with fries, macaroni and cheese and pita pizza. These cost between $4.50 and $8, not including a drink (sodas are $3.95) or a child's dessert ($4) such as a brownie or ice cream sundae. When you make your reservation, if you mention that your child will be celebrating a birthday or a special occasion, a trio of beautiful multicolored balloons will be waiting at the table. And don't forget your camera — you might as well act like a tourist, everyone else here does.

KIDS EAT NEW YORK

THE AMERICAN MUSEUM
OF NATURAL HISTORY
79th St. & Central Park West

....

(General Information: 769-5100
   IMAX: 769-5034

TRANSPORTATION:

🚇 B,C to 81st St.;
   1,2,3,9 to 79th St.

Parking:

The Museum Parking Lot, located at W. 81st St.
between Columbus Ave. & CPW, is temporarily
closed. Please call 769-5606 to see if reopened
or for alternative parking. When open, the parking
lot hours are 7 AM - 11:30 PM, with an hourly fee
upto a $17 daily maximum.

General Museum Hours:
Sun-Thurs: 10 AM - 5:45 PM
Fri/Sat: 10 AM - 8:45 PM

Nature Science Center Hours: (769-5310)
Tue-Fri: 2 - 4:30 PM
Sat & Sun: 1 - 4:30 PM
Thu Storytelling: 3 PM

Discovery Room Hours:
Sat & Sun: 12 noon - 4:30 PM

Museum Admission:
Adults - $8; Students & Seniors - $6;
Kids (2-12) - $4.50
Note: Some exhibitions have an additional fee,
usually $2.50 to 5.00.

IMAX Admission: (includes Museum admission)
Adults - $12; Seniors & Student - $8.50;
Kids (2-12) - $6.50

Note: The Planetarium is closed for renovations
until 1999-2000.

The Museum of Natural History, with more than forty exhibition halls, is one of our frequent museum destinations. A resource for every child of the city (as well as adults and visitors), it includes many wonderful displays. We suggest, however, that you limit your visits with children to two or three hours, otherwise the museum can feel overwhelming and the floors very hard. We especially enjoy the first- and second-floor dioramas (realistic renderings of creatures in their natural settings), and the Dinosaur halls. There are two rooms specifically set up for kids: The 1st floor Discovery Room, and the 2nd floor Natural Science Center, which is a living science exhibit run by the Education Department that includes plants, insects, and animals. Other halls you won't want to miss are Human Biology and Evolution; Mammals and Their Extinct Relatives (featuring the gigantic woolly mammoth), and Ocean Life, (with its monster-looking deep-sea fish and life-sized blue whale). The Imax theater presents films that are both interesting and educational.

Three restaurants are located in the museum: The Garden Cafe, Diner Saurus and the Whale's Lair. On Saturdays and Sundays from 11 AM to 4 PM snack carts are also located at the 77th Street entrance, near the big canoe and the Human Biology Exhibit.

GARDEN CAFE
Lower Level
American Museum of Natural History
Use Central Park West stairs or elevators.

(769-5865

Hours:
Lunch:
Mon-Fri: 11:30 AM - 3:30 PM
Dinner:
Fri & Sat: 5 - 7:30 PM
Brunch:
Sat & Sun: 11 AM - 4 PM

\$\$ **Entertainment:** Museum, menu coloring

A pretty sunroom overlooking the garden, with green and red cafe tables, upholstered chairs, and botanical prints, the Garden Cafe is a nice place to go to for a civilized meal, especially if the grandparents are along. The restaurant is very family-friendly. The crayon-ready $6.95 dinosaur kids' menu offers pizza, chicken nuggets, burgers, hot dogs, and grilled cheese, all with fries and a choice of milk juice, or soda. The crayons are supplied for free.

The full menu consists of entrees (average $12) such as salmon or chicken, pastas, soups, salads, sandwiches, and burgers. The lunch specials ($13.50) and dinner specials ($15.95) are worth considering. Wine and beer are available. There is also a dinner package ($24 for adults, $13 for kids) that includes an Imax double-feature admission. To make reservations, you have to call the general information line and wade through the automated calling system until you reach the restaurant option.

DINER SAURUS
FAST SERVICE EATERY

Lower Level
American Museum of Natural History
Use the Central Park West stairs or elevators.

📞 769-5865

Hours:
11 AM - 4:45 PM (strict closing)
Brunch: No

     Entertainment: Museum

This is a clean fast-food eatery that is a perfect pit stop for kids. It offers regular and veggie burgers, fries, pizza, dogs, salads, and sandwiches such as ham and Swiss, chicken, and tuna fish. There are also brownies, ice cream, milk, juice, sodas, and coffee.

WHALE'S LAIR

1st floor Ocean Life Hall
American Museum of Natural History

Hours:
Fri: 3 - 7:30 PM
Sat: 12 noon - 7:30 PM
Sun & most holidays:
12 noon - 4 PM
Brunch: No

 \$ **Entertainment:** Museum

The Whale's Lair is a sixty-seat snack bar located directly under the big whale. Open daily, this is a good place for snacks like pretzels or an easy meal of hot dogs, soups, sandwiches, and salads. Beverages include sodas, juice and coffee. There are also desserts.

Near to the Museum are several nice restaurants that could provide the perfect lunch or dinner to go along with your museum visit:

EJ's LUNCHEONETTE 477 Amsterdam Ave.
(between 81st & 82nd Sts.) 873-3444
ISOLA 485 Columbus Ave.
(between 83rd & 84th Sts.) 362-7400
MAIN STREET 446 Columbus Ave.
(between 81st & 82nd Sts.) 873-5025
MUSEUM CAFE 66 Columbus Ave.
(at 77th St.) 799-0150
PATSY'S PIZZA 61 W. 74th St.
(at Columbus Ave.) 579-3000
POPOVER CAFE 551 Amsterdam Ave.
(between 86th & 87th Sts.) 595-8555
SARABETH'S 423 Amsterdam Ave.
(between 80th & 81st Sts.) 496-6280

SPECIAL ATTRACTIONS FOR KIDS
with nearby
RESTAURANT RECOMMENDATIONS
(Great attractions that <u>don't</u> have on-location
restaurants)
••

AMERICAN CRAFT MUSEUM
956-3535 Midtown
40 W. 53rd St. (between 5th & 6th Aves.)

CENTRAL PARK BELVEDERE CASTLE & SWEDISH COTTAGE
772-0210 Midpark (at 79th St.)

CENTRAL PARK CAROUSEL & DAIRY
879-0244 Midpark (at 64th St.)

KIDS EAT NEW YORK

MICKEY MANTLE'S **196**
PATSY'S PIZZERIA **248**
PEPPERMINT PARK **250**
SERENDIPITY 3 **253**

CENTRAL PARK CHILDREN'S ZOO
861-6030   5th Ave. at 64th St. (Central Park East)

CALIFORNIA PIZZA KITCHEN **230**
JACKSON HOLE **242**
THE JEKYLL & HYDE CLUB **188**
JOHN'S PIZZERIA **288**
MICKEY MANTLE'S **196**
PEPPERMINT PARK **250**
SERENDIPITY 3 **253**

CHILDREN'S MUSEUM OF THE ARTS
274-0986   SoHo
72 Spring St. (between Broadway & Lafayette Sts.)

IL CORALLO TRATTORIA **62**
KELLEY & PING **64**
LOMBARDI'S **66**
SOHO KITCHEN & BAR **71**
TENNESSEE MOUNTAIN **73**

CHILDREN'S MUSEUM OF MANHATTAN
721-1234   Upper West Side
212 W. 83rd St. (between Broadway & Amsterdam Ave.)

BOULEVARD **275**
ERNIE'S **280**
E.J.'S LUNCHEONETTE **278**
GOOD ENOUGH TO EAT **282**
ISOLA **284**
JACKSON HOLE **286**
MAIN STREET **289**
MARY ANN'S **291**
NOVA GRILL **296**
OLLIE'S NOODLE SHOP & GRILLE **298**
POPOVER CAFE **301**
SARABETH'S **303**

SPECIAL ATTRACTIONS INDEX

KIDS EAT NEW YORK

MOONROCK DINER **198**
MOTOWN CAFE **199**
PLANET HOLLYWOOD **202**
TELEVISION CITY **207**

FORBES MUSEUM
206-5548 Greenwich Village
62 5th Ave. (at 12th St.)

BAYAMO **80**
CHAT 'N CHEW **129**
E.J.'S LUNCHEONETTE **86**
ELEPHANT & CASTLE **88**
PATSY'S PIZZERIA **105**
TSUNAMI **115**
WORLD ROOM **150**

FORBIDDEN PLANET
473-1576 Greenwich Village
840 Broadway (at 13th St.)

AMERICA **126**
BAYAMO **80**
CHAT 'N CHEW **129**
E.J.'S LUNCHEONETTE **86**
ELEPHANT & CASTLE **88**
PATSY'S PIZZERIA **105**
WORLD ROOM **150**

GUGGENHEIM MUSEUM SOHO
344-5330 SoHo
575 Broadway (at Prince St.)

BAYAMO **80**
CUPPING ROOM CAFE **60**
IL CORALLO TRATTORIA **62**
KELLEY & PING **64**
LOMBARDI'S **66**
SILVER SPURS **110**
SOHO KITCHEN & BAR **71**
TENNESSEE MOUNTAIN **73**

SPECIAL ATTRACTIONS INDEX

INFOQUEST CENTER, AT&T BUILDING

615-5555 Midtown

550 Madison (at 56th St.)

INTERNATIONAL CENTER OF PHOTOGRAPHY

860-1777 Upper East Side

1130 5th Ave. (at 94th St.)

INTREPID SEA AIR SPACE MUSEUM

245-0072 Midtown

Pier 86, W. 46th St. (at 12th Ave./West Side Highway) Note: Almost all are a cab ride away.

KIDS EAT NEW YORK

JEWISH MUSEUM
423-3200 Upper East Side
1109 5th Ave. (at 92nd St.)

BARKING DOG LUNCHEONETTE **225**
BROTHER JIMMY'S BAIT SHACK **229**
JACKSON HOLE **242**
SARABETH'S **251**
VINEGAR FACTORY RESTAURANT **257**
YURA & COMPANY **258**

LINCOLN CENTER
FOR THE PERFORMING ARTS
875-5000 West Side
W. 65th Street & Broadway
(Note: Most suggestions are a long walk
or a short cab ride away.)

BROOKLYN DINER **164**
DALLAS BBQ **277**
HARD ROCK CAFE **179**
JOHN'S PIZZERIA **288**
MICKEY MANTLE'S **196**
PLANET HOLLYWOOD **202**
TAVERN ON THE GREEN **305**

LOWER EAST SIDE
TENEMENT MUSEUM
431-0233 Little Italy/SoHo
97 Orchard St. (between Broome & Delancey Sts.)

CUPPING ROOM CAFE **60**
IL CORALLO TRATTORIA **62**
KATZ'S DELI **93**
KELLEY & PING **64**
LOMBARDI'S **66**
SECOND KOSHER AVENUE DELI **108**
SOHO KITCHEN & BAR **71**
TENNESSEE MOUNTAIN **73**

SPECIAL ATTRACTIONS INDEX

MUSEUM OF THE CITY OF NEW YORK

534-1672 Upper East Side
5th Ave. at 103rd St.
Note: All these restaurants are a short taxi ride away.

BARKING DOG LUNCHEONETTE **225**
BROTHER JIMMY'S BAIT SHACK **229**
JACKSON HOLE **242**
SARABETH'S **251**
VINEGAR FACTORY RESTAURANT **257**
YURA & COMPANY **258**

MUSEUM OF TV AND RADIO

621-6800 Midtown
25 W. 52nd St. (between 5th & 6th Aves.)

BENIHANA OF TOKYO **162**
BROOKLYN DINER **164**
CAFE UN DEUX TROIS **168**
ELLEN'S STARDUST DINER **174**
FASHION CAFE **175**
HARD ROCK CAFE **179**
HARLEY DAVIDSON CAFE **181**
THE JEKYLL & HYDE CLUB **188**
LUCKY'S BAR & GRILL **192**
MICKEY MANTLE'S **196**
MOTOWN CAFE **199**
PLANET HOLLYWOOD **202**
TELEVISION CITY **207**

NATIONAL MUSEUM OF THE AMERICAN INDIAN (Division of the Smithsonian Museum) 668-2623

Downtown 1 Bowling Green
(at South Ferry, Battery Park City,
in the Old Customs Building)

EDWARD MORAN BAR & GRILL **53**
ELLEN'S CAFE AND BAKE SHOP **24**
HAMBURGER HARRY'S **27**
PIPELINE **54**

KIDS EAT NEW YORK

NEW YORK STOCK EXCHANGE
656-5168 Downtown 20 Broad St.

ELLEN'S CAFE AND BAKE SHOP **24**

HAMBURGER HARRY'S **27**

SOUTH STREET SEAPORT 19 Fulton St. at the East
River (See separate South Street Seaport listing).
Restaurants included are:

   CAFE FLEDERMAUS **44**

   FULTON STREET CAFE **43**

   LIBERTY CAFE & OYSTER BAR **38**

   PEDRO O'HARA'S **41**

   SEQUOIA **39**

   SGARLATO'S CAFE **40**

See separate World Financial Center listing.
Restaurants included are:

   EDWARD MORAN BAR & GRILL **53**

   PIPELINE **54**

NYC FIRE DEPT. MUSEUM
691-1303 SoHo
278 Spring St. (between Hudson & Varick Sts.)

CUPPING ROOM CAFE **60**

IL CORALLO TRATTORIA **62**

KELLEY & PING **64**

SILVER SPURS **70**

SOHO KITCHEN & BAR **71**

RADIO CITY MUSIC HALL
632-4041 Midtown
1260 6th Ave. (between 50th & 51st Sts.)

ALL STAR CAFE, OFFICIAL **160**

BENIHANA OF TOKYO **162**

BROOKLYN DINER **164**

CAFE UN DEUX TROIS **168**

ELLEN'S STARDUST DINER **174**

FASHION CAFE **175**

HAMBURGER HARRY'S **177**

HARD ROCK CAFE **179**

HARLEY DAVIDSON CAFE **181**

THE JEKYLL & HYDE CLUB **188**

KIDS EAT NEW YORK

OLLIE'S NOODLE SHOP & GRILLE **201**
SKYLIGHT DINER **204**
STARDUST DINE-O-MAT **206**
TELEVISION CITY **207**
VIRGIL'S REAL BBQ **209**

TIMES SQUARE
Broadway & 42nd St. (See Theatre District.)

WARNER BROS. STUDIO STORE
754-0300 Midtown
1 E. 57th St. (at 5th Ave.)

BENIHANA OF TOKYO **162**
BROOKLYN DINER **164**
ELLEN'S STARDUST DINER **174**
FASHION CAFE **175**
HARD ROCK CAFE **179**
HARLEY DAVIDSON CAFE **181**
THE JEKYLL & HYDE CLUB **188**
LUCKY'S BAR & GRILL **192**
MOONROCK DINER **198**
MICKEY MANTLE'S **196**
MOTOWN CAFE **199**
PLANET HOLLYWOOD **202**
TELEVISION CITY **207**

WONDERCAMP
243-1111 Chelsea
27 W. 23rd St. (between 5th & 6th Aves.)

AMERICA **126**
BENDIX DINER **128**
HOT TOMATO **140**
MAYROSE **144**
TWIGS **149**

INDEX CATEGORIES:

••

BBQ RESTAURANTS

FOR BOYS: 7-12 YEARS OLD

KIDS EAT NEW YORK

KID'S MENU

DINERS, DELIS & COFFEE SHOPS

KIDS EAT NEW YORK

ENTERTAINMENT
(beyond coloring books)

ETHNIC RESTAURANTS

(not including Italian)

FREE KID'S MEALS

(See reviews for conditions)

KIDS EAT NEW YORK

FOR GIRLS: 7-12 YEARS OLD

FOR GRANDPARENTS, WITH KIDS

KIDS EAT NEW YORK

PIZZA SERVED

KIDS EAT NEW YORK

KIDS EAT NEW YORK

ALPHABETICAL
RESTAURANT LIST

KIDS EAT NEW YORK

KIDS EAT NEW YORK

ABOUT THE AUTHORS

· ·

SAM FREUND

Sam turned eleven in 1997. He lives in New York City. Besides eating out and traveling, Sam loves to play miniature golf and go to the movies, the beach, and the many playgrounds in Manhattan. His interests include drawing, acting and make-believe, reading, and writing stories. When he is not busy playing with his friends, he likes to play computer and video games.

ELIZABETH CARPENTER

Sam's mother Elizabeth is an artist and fashion designer who owns and operates an independent design studio in the Flatiron district of Manhattan. Her work has allowed her to travel extensively throughout Europe, Africa, and Asia. Elizabeth's interests are designing, painting and illustration, photography, and travel.